THE SOUND OF HOLY

a collection of poetry and art

AMY MARIE LANGE

The Sound of Holy: a collection of poetry and art

Artwork: Amy Lange

Published by Seraph Creative in 2025

United States / United Kingdom / South Africa / Australia

www.seraphcreative.org

ISBN 978-1-964959-83-2 (hardcover)

ISBN 978-1-964959-70-2 (paperback)

eBook 978-1-964959-71-9

I dedicate this book to the two most precious kisses from heaven...my two children—Rafael and Selah.

You radiate the realms
with your laughter and giggles.
You crack open the darkest
of hearts with one smile.
Heaven sings and creation dances
in awe of your wonder.
You embody the Father's heart
with your resilience,
gentleness, carefreeness,
laughter and silliness,
and tenderness which
bursts like confetti
wherever you step.

I am honored that the Father chose me as your mom.
I love you Rafael and Selah.
-Momma

Contents

IN AMY'S OWN WORDS:

"This collection of poems and artwork are very personal. Raw. Very sacred to me. I'm opening a page of my journal with Yeshua and inviting you in—to dine with Him. I've carried these words quietly for a long time, and I'm ready to share them with the world. My prayer is that it becomes a sacred space for you—that in reading, you wouldn't just read or flip through these pages, but instead engage with His sound and heart for you — that you would encounter Your Bridegroom... that heaven will brush close to you and take you in. Deeper. That the sound of holy would echo and awaken your heart."

FOREWORD

The Sound of Holy will effortlessly open hidden anterooms in the back corners of your mind. The colorfully crafted word pictures herein, will insert rare keys of rhema into those locked doors. Doors which may have gotten locked for myriad possible reasons. The lyrics of these musings will sometimes spill through your mind as forceful as a stormy gale. And at other times, as soft as the zephyrs of a butterfly's wings. Amy's insights come from the vibrant artesian springs of a creative. You'll appreciate the depth behind the word phrases and be mesmerized by the inspiring mixed media which accompanies most of these poems and prose. You'll find that although Amy Lange is quite gifted in applying colors and overlays on the surface of the canvas, she is also gifted in 'painting' life-giving pictures on the canvas of your mind and heart. You'll have a greater appreciation for beauty and be a more beautiful person for reading *The Sound of Holy*.

Mark Hendrickson
www.dpmkc.org
Author of Supernatural Provision

Hear His sound

A Love Letter from Yeshua

Hello My Darling,

I've been waiting for this moment for a long time. Will you let go of all that distracts you and take My hand?

Come away with Me. I am waiting for you. Go ahead, find a quiet place where the world cannot follow us. Shut the door and find a cozy place to sit. I Am here. I Am holding this space and time for us. Just breathe deep, and let all the noise fall away— I want you here, with Me.

I have been longing for this moment when nothing stands between us. Let Me draw you into My dance. Invite My Spirit near—He knows what your heart aches for.

I Am closer than your breath. Do you hear My sound? I Am slowing everything down for a moment. Just take a moment to breathe in My presence. I Am your breath.

I Am taking you deeper within Me—My place of rest...where striving ends and My love becomes your everything.

These pages are your sacred space where I will envelope you and take you deeper.

I love you,

Yeshua

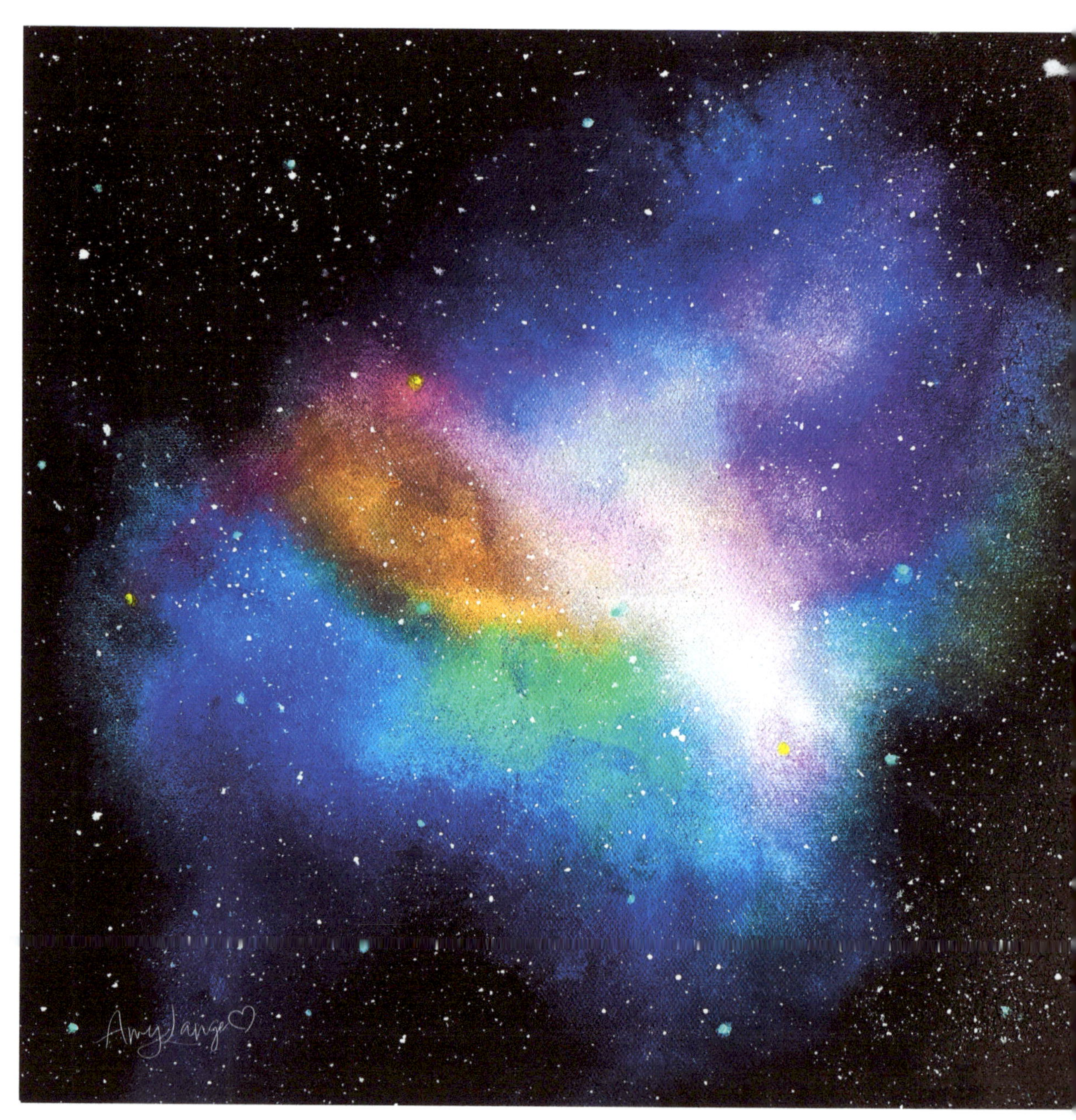

"Echoes of Light" *acrylic on canvas*

echoes of light

In the beginning God created the heavens and the earth. The earth was unformed and void, darkness was on the face of the deep, and the Spirit of God hovered over the surface of the water. Then God said, "Let there be light"; and there was light. God saw that the light was good, and God divided the light from the darkness.
Genesis 1:1-4

Here, in the deep—
where no foot falls
and silence reigns—
I hear gentle ripples
echoing "Light".

Vibrations
shimmer
around me,
soft with love.
Then suddenly
I become
enveloped in
Your exhale
within the dark.

Flames flicker
at Your breath.
Silence suddenly
is lit with
knowing—
and in the hush,
each star
becomes a word,
a vibration,
a symphony
of Your
wonder
veiled
in color.

I drift—
steadied
by Your eye
as the ancients
of wisdom
winds,
drawing me
closer
to where
I belong.

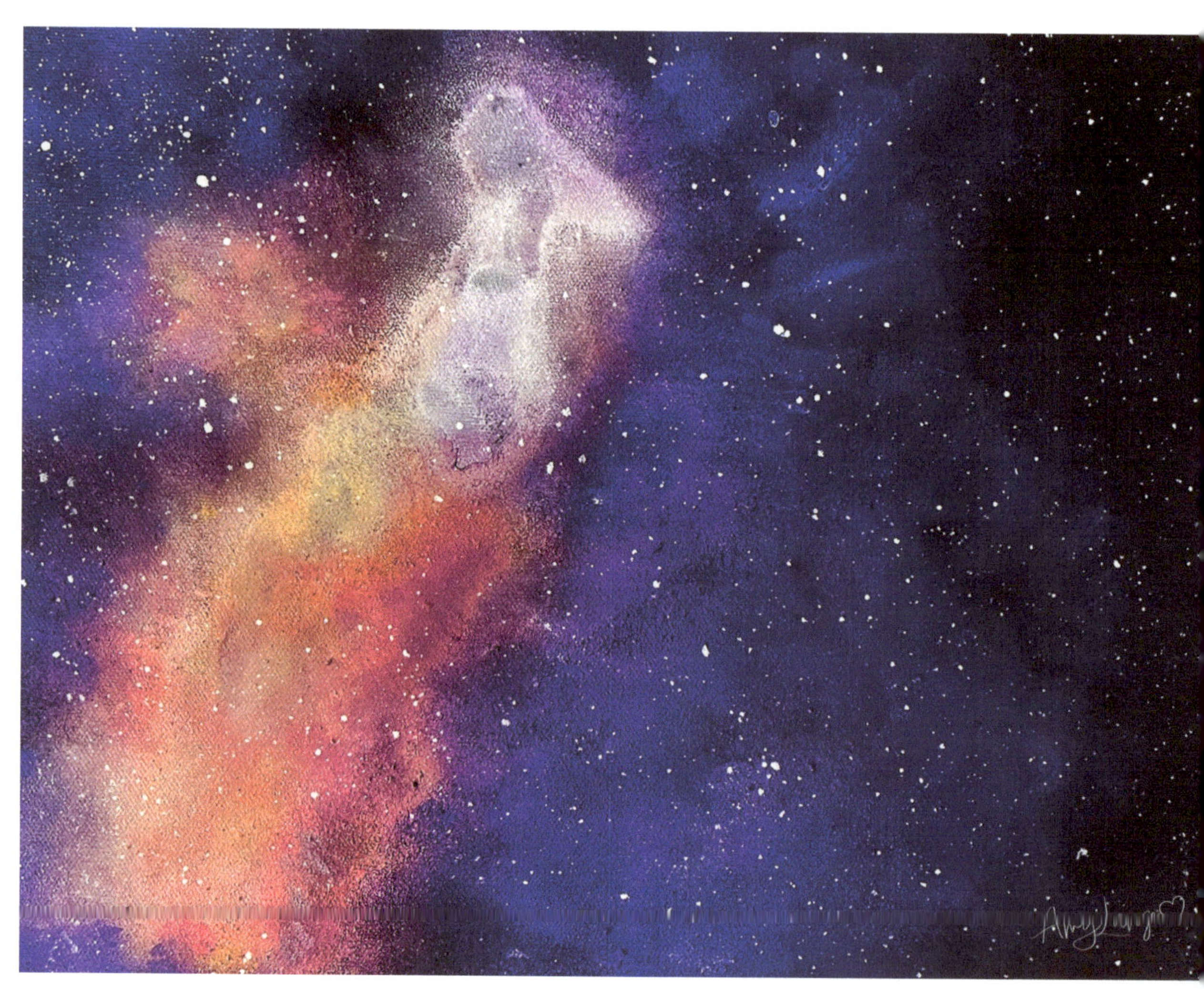

"Cradle of Light" *acrylic on canvas*

cradle of light

Rise up in splendor and be radiant, for your light has dawned, and Yahweh's glory now streams from you! Look carefully! Darkness blankets the earth, and thick clouds covers the nations, but Yahweh arises upon you and the brightness of his glory appears over you!
Isaiah 60:1-2

Oh, wise
in heart
consuming
flame,
lightning
flashes
at Your
Name.

Glory
veiled, divine
and deep,
I step inside
where secrets
keep.

Adorned
in beauty,
twined
within,
woven
tightly—
no loose
ends.

Your palm
surrounds,
with light
and sound,
in Your
story,
I am
found.

One to sixty,
a spark
draws near,
creation
from void,
all things
made
clear.

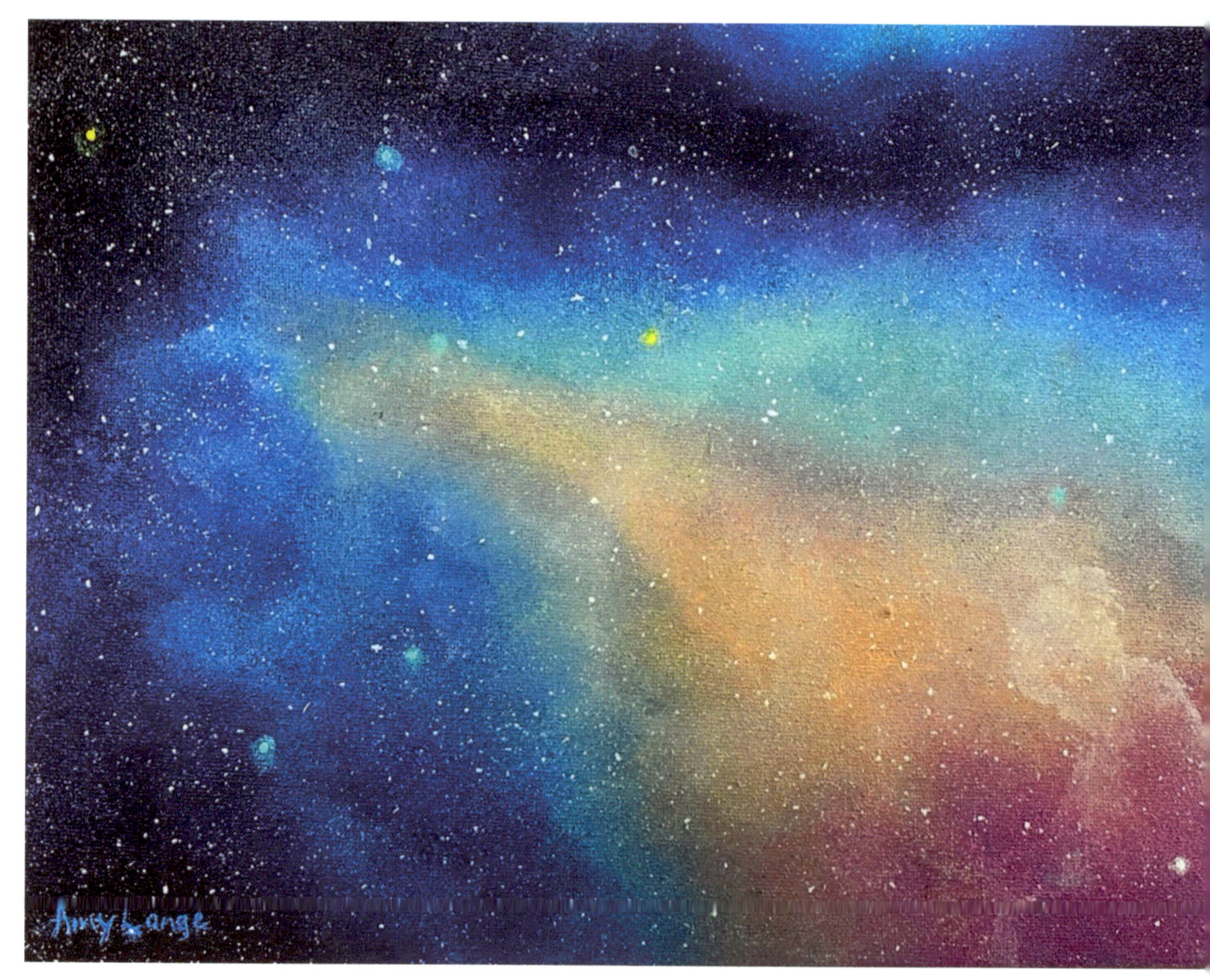

"Whispers" *acrylic on canvas*

In the void
before the song,
Yahweh's breath
made light
to dawn.

Stars awoke
in silent praise,
Nebulas
burned with
holy gaze.

Yet within this
cosmic sweep,
my heart
is bowed with
yielded knee.

A whispered
groan comes
from the deep–
it finds
Your ear;
a flowing
stream.

For You who
paint the
endless skies
still gathers
tears from
weary
eyes.

Galaxies turn,
yet You
draw near.

My Abba listens,
my Abba hears.

whispers

Call to Me and I will answer you, and tell you [and even show you] great and mighty things, [things which have been confined and hidden], which you do not know and understand and cannot distinguish.
Jeremiah 33:3

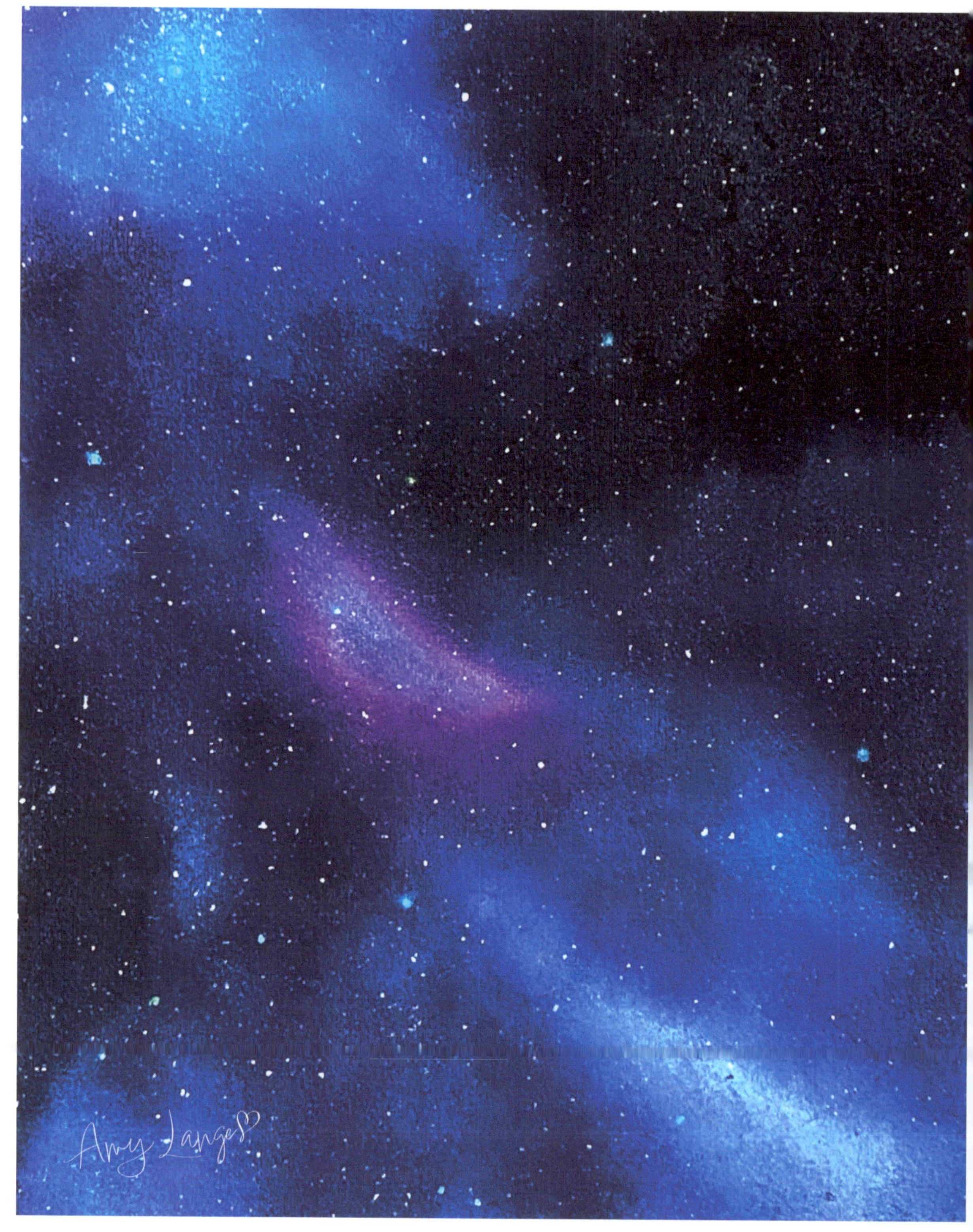

"The Dance" *acrylic on canvas*

the dance

Because of You, I know the path of life, as I taste the fullness of joy in Your presence. At Your right side I experience divine pleasures forevermore!
Psalms 16:11

Your breath beckons me
in the silence
before the world awakes.

You call. I don't hesitate. I can't.
Something in me knows
it's all You or nothing.

The darkness is thick in time–
but I walk.
Each step is breaking something
I thought I needed.

My heart is filled with why's.
You don't explain. You just lead me
to the thru.

Trusting You. Your wind winds.
You take me In.

Stillness. All around.
The air is breathing.
Heavy with something ancient.

My steps continue
because I want You
more than answers.

I feel You in the path, in the ache,
in the pull with each step.

Suddenly Your storm of love
rushes thru me. Not gentle.
It wrecks me in the best way.

I can't hold it.
So I just let You flood me.

I drink. I break. I breathe.
I'm Yours.

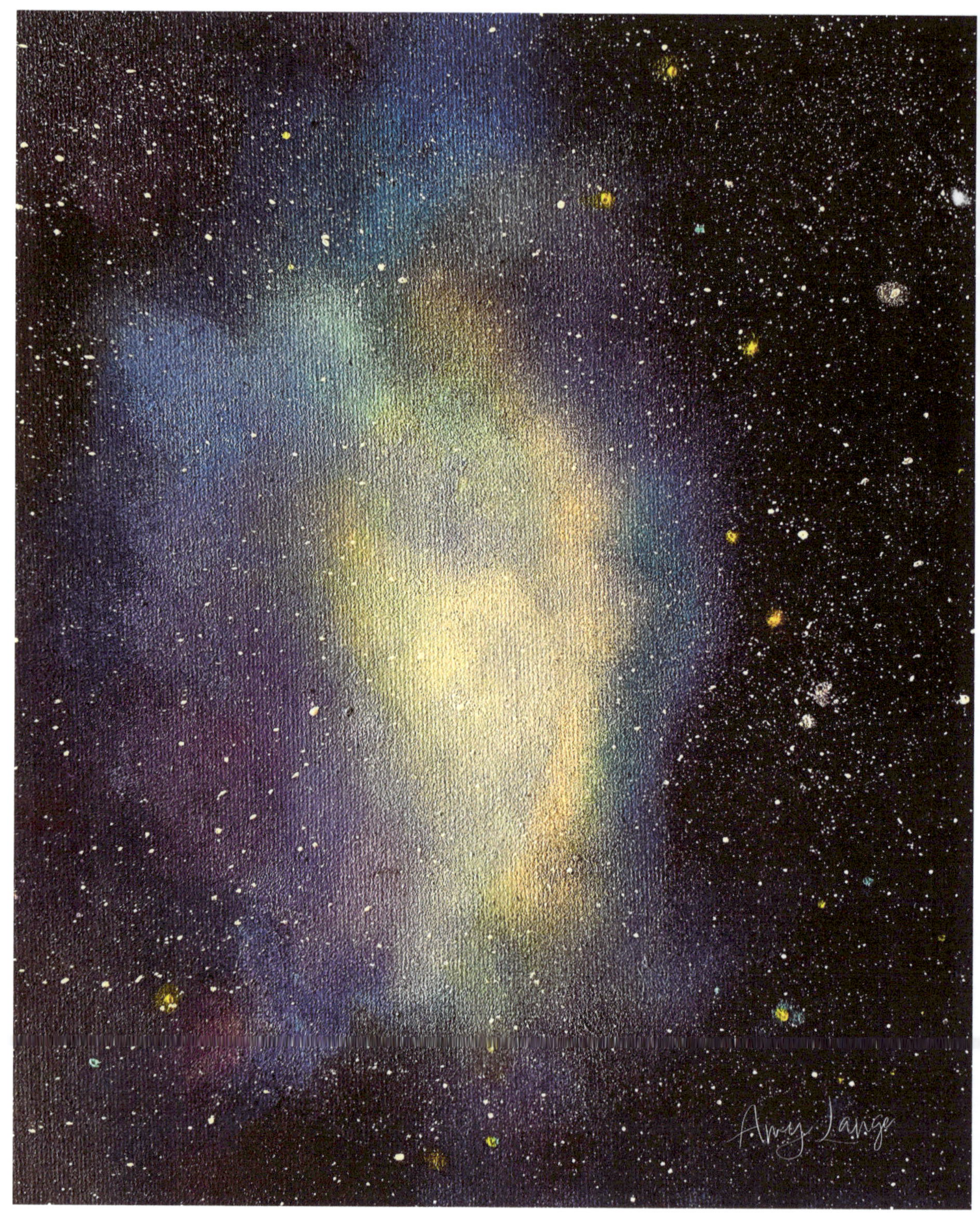

"Wrapped in Love" *acrylic on canvas*

footsteps of wisdom

Listen to my counsel, for my instruction will enlighten you. You'll be wise not to ignore it. If you wait at wisdom's doorway, longing to hear a word for every day, joy will break forth within you as you listen for what I'll say. For the fountain of life pours into you every time that you find me, and this is the secret of growing in the delight and the favor of the Lord.
Proverbs 8:33-35

I am the breath of being,
the pulse of endless skies,
a keeper of untold secrets,
a flame that never dies.

I pierce the soul with radiance,
and light what lies unknown.
I kindle hope in shadows
where dreams are overthrown.

I am soft, yet deeply stirring,
a fire both fierce and kind,
I soothe the restless yearning
and awaken heart and mind.

My treasures gleam in silence,
my path is sharp and steep.
Will you bear the weight of wonder
and the mysteries that I keep?

I dwell within the stillness,
wrapped in unyielding light.
I guide you through the chaos,
and silence endless nights.

My love burns bright with passion,
my joy is vast, divine.
I blaze beyond all boundaries,
a mirror to all time.

I call the lost and broken,
the bold, the weak, the meek—
"Come closer, will you find me?
Will you dare to truly seek?"

Feast upon my whispers,
drink deeply of my peace.
For the faithful, I unravel
wonders that never cease.

Will you leave behind your comfort?
Will you bear the final cost?
I stand before you waiting,
for what's hidden and what's lost.

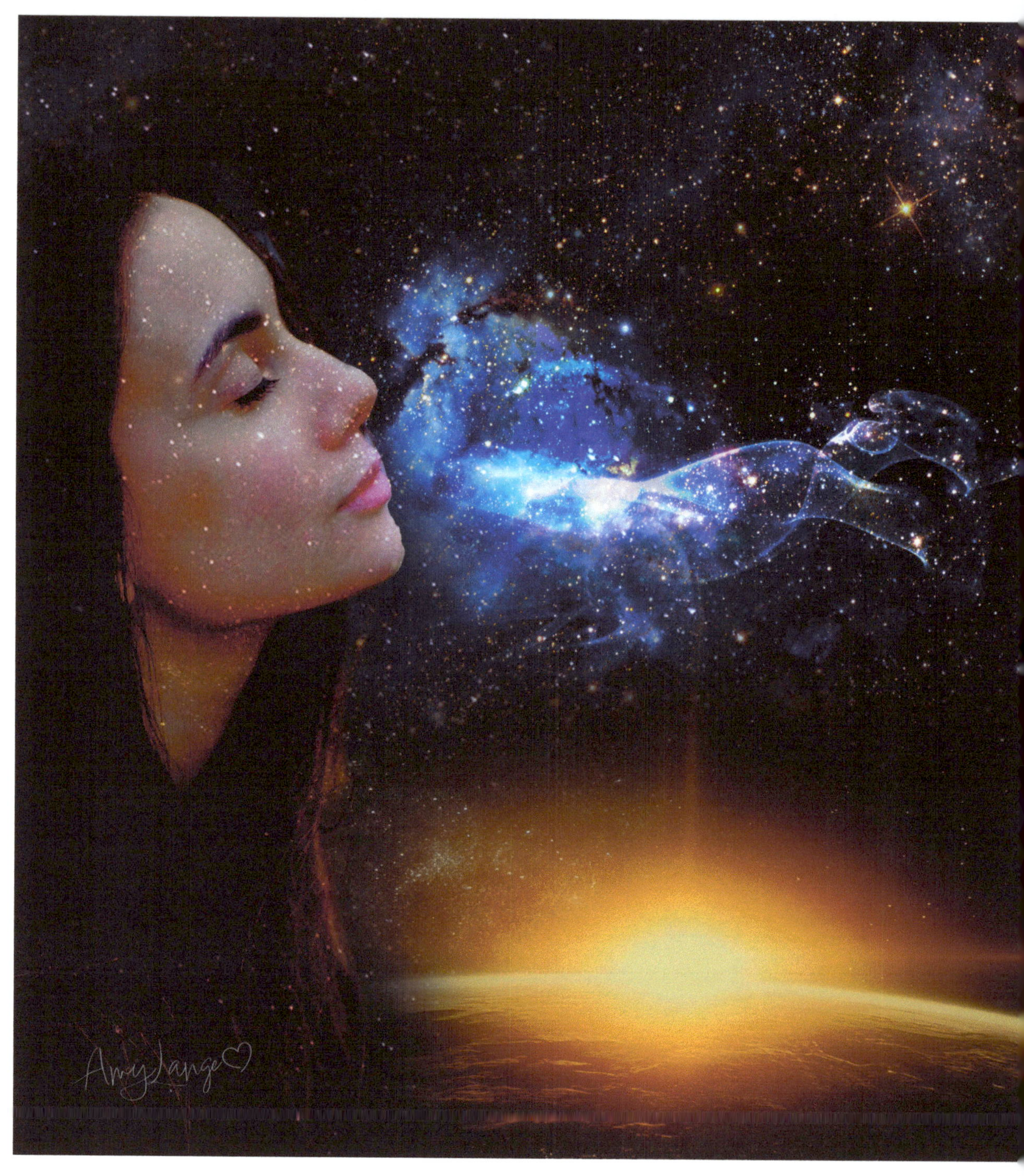

"Sacred Breath" *digital media*

Sacred breath

In the beginning God created the heavens and the earth. Now the earth was chaos and waste, darkness was on the surface of the deep, and the Ruach Elohim was hovering upon the surface of the water. Then God said, "Let there be light!" and there was light.
Genesis 1:1-3

As I sit in stillness,
I reflect on the moment
You spoke—
and it all began.

Your breath
escaped with pause,
Inhale... Echad held all.
Exhale...creation was born.

What was the color
of Your breath
in that first divine release?
Uncovered treasures
wrapped in light?

Did diamonds scatter
across the void?
Did precious gems
rain through Your
heavenly dome?

What song did the angels sing
as silence broke in wonder?

Did Your breath carry a holy hush,
a sound too sacred for words?

What was that sacred moment—
when breath became stars,
and the universe inhaled
the sound of life?

A sacred breath that
whispers gently,
holds tightly,
encircles intently,
gazing always.

The breath that filled the stars,
now fills the silence
in me, whispering always...
"Let there be..."

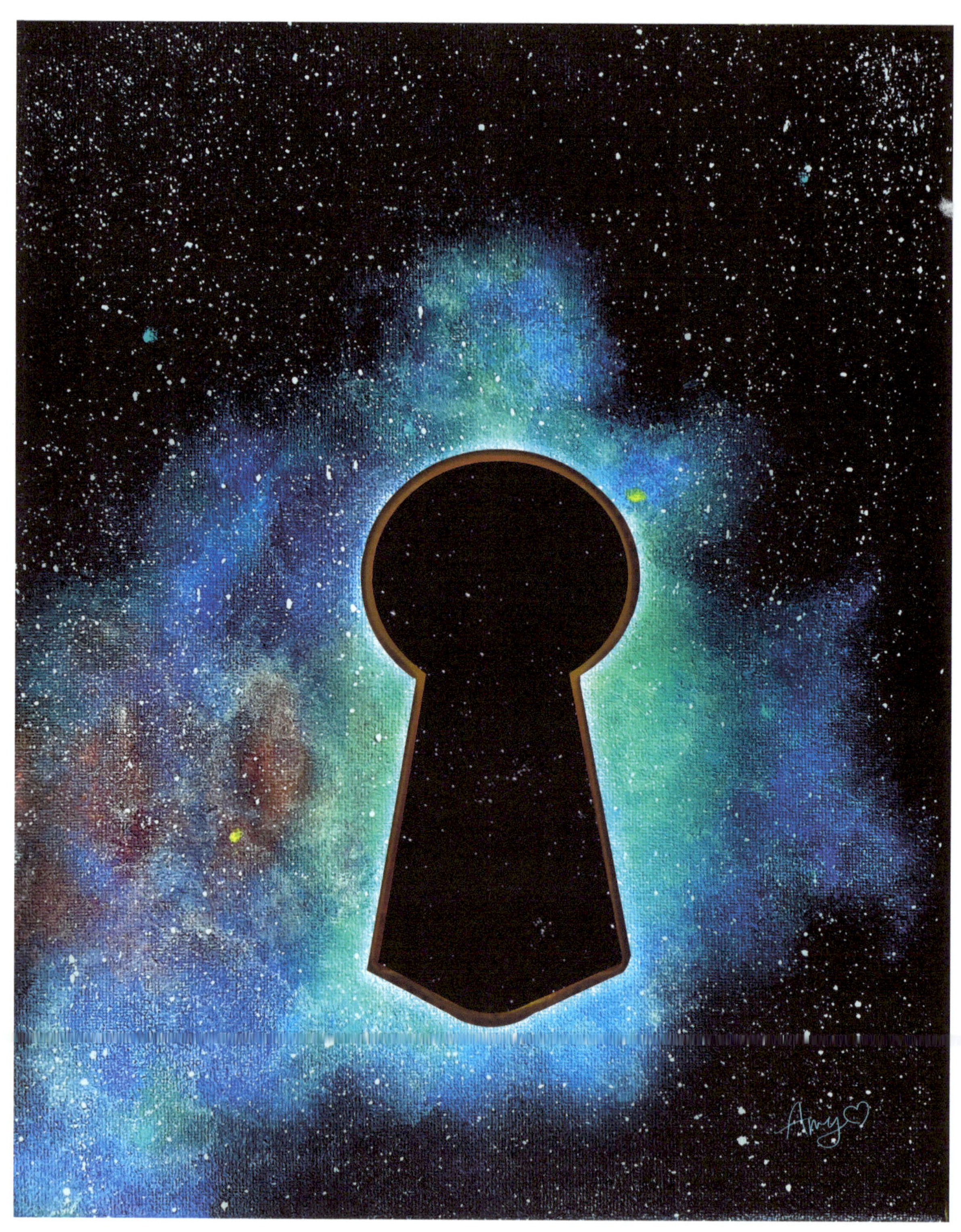

"Within" *mixed media*

Within my heart,
there lies a door—
unlike the rest,
yet made for more.

Not forged in gold,
nor shaped by hand,
it holds no age,
no time, no land.

This door is ancient,
wild and wide—
the breath before
the stars aligned.

"Unlock My heart,
turn the key,
all who hunger,
come and see..."

Beyond the veil
of silent space,
destiny stirs
in blazing grace.

Mysteries unfold
within your heart.
Just turn and face
His sacred knock.

What lies beyond
the shadowed fold
is stirred by faith
and hearts made bold.

within

Behold, I'm standing at the door, knocking. If your heart is open to hear my voice and you open the door within, I will come in to you and feast with you, and you will feast with me.
Revelation 3:20

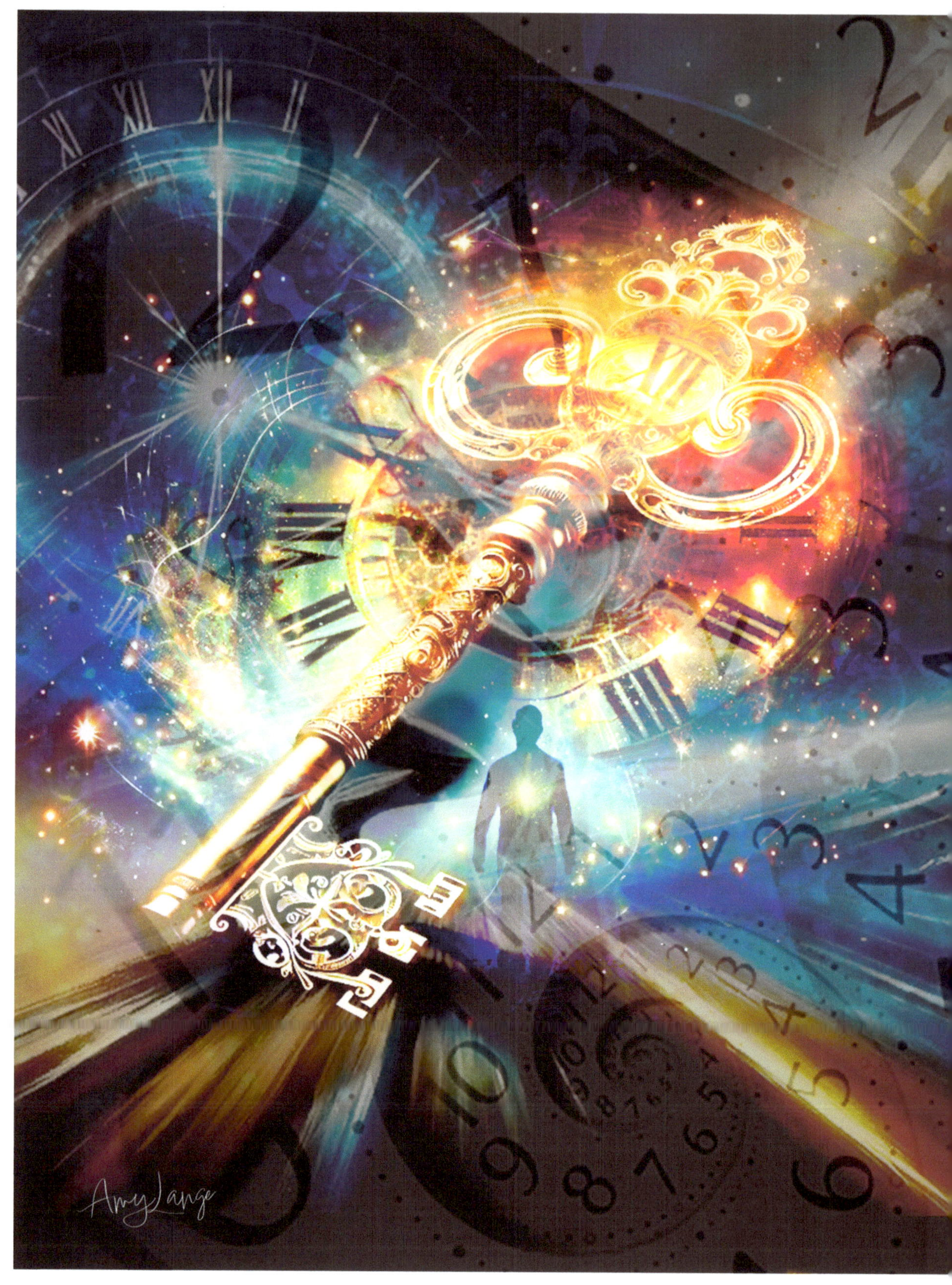

“Awakened” *digital media*

awakened

Stop dwelling on the past. Don't even remember these former things. I am doing something brand new, something unheard of. Even now it sprouts and grows and matures. Don't you perceive it? I will make a way in the wilderness and open up flowing streams in the desert. Isaiah 43:18-19

Awakening is never as you think
Resembling darkness instead of Light.

In isolation,
ears open,
faith deepens,
spirit quickens,
heaven broods.

In preparation there is
stretching, refinement
stripping, polishing.

To the natural eye
all looks lost.
Rejection.
Failure.
Uncertainty.
Confusion.

But peer closer, see beyond...
See with His eyes.
Redirection, preservation,
deliverance, from settling.

Your not off course, your guided
by His divine hand.

Embrace the pain.
Destiny lies in Him—not man.

Crowning comes with opposition,
resistance, shifting.

You're not weak, your dangerous.
Aligned with His agenda.
Identity rising—fire blazing.
No derailment, only unveiling.

Awakened.

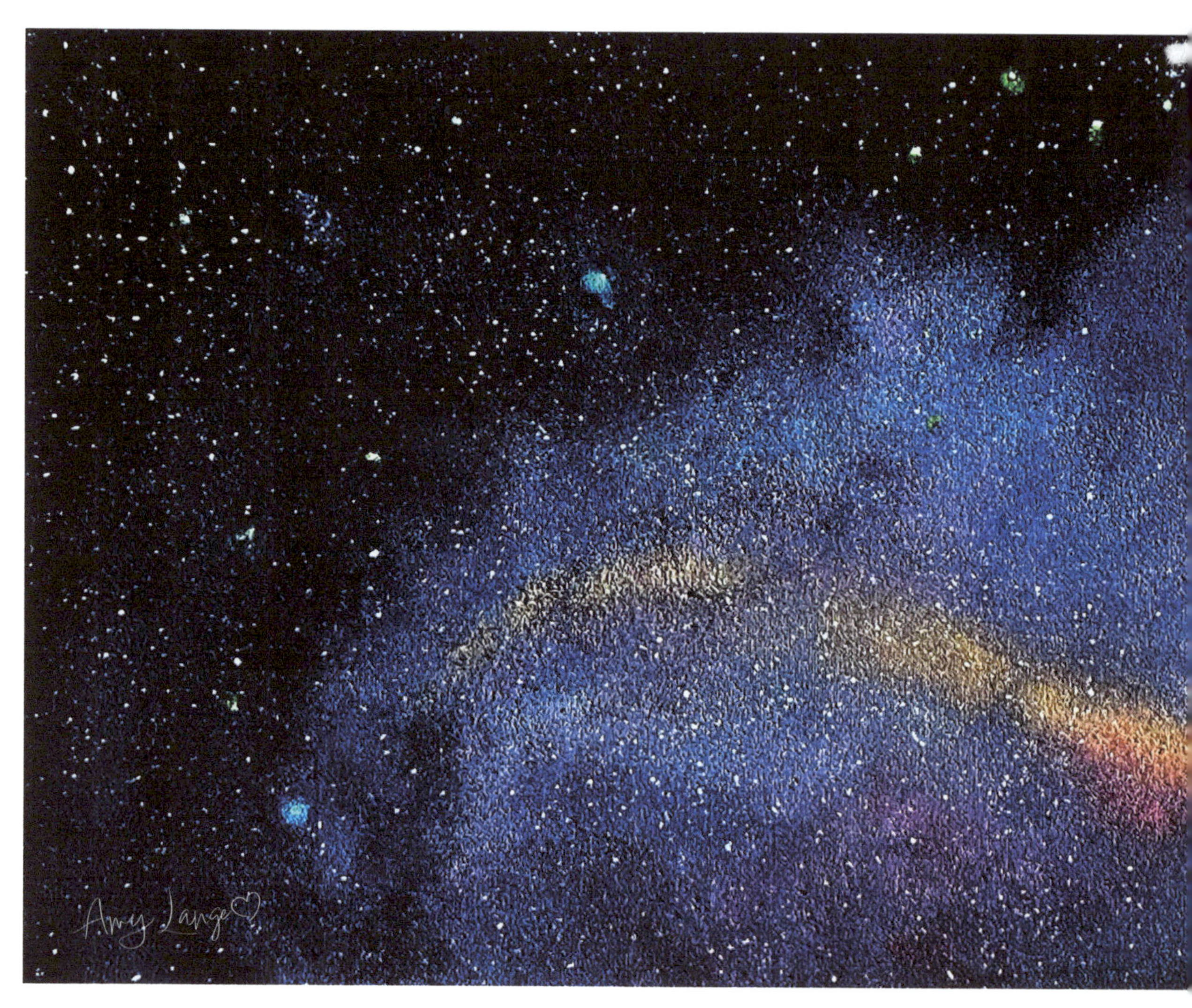

"Joy and Wonder" *acrylic on canvas*

joy and wonder

"[You are the One] who covers Yourself with light as with a garment, Who stretches out the heavens like a tent curtain, Who lays the beams of His upper chambers in the waters [above the firmament], Who makes the clouds His chariot, Who walks on the wings of the wind, Who makes winds His messengers, Flames of fire His ministers. [Heb 1:7]" Psalms 104:2-4

I journey deeper,
step by step,
into Your heart.
A boundless expanse
where eternity starts.

You fill my eyes
with wonder, a holy gaze,
Your beauty ignites
my utmost praise.

To love You is to see it all
unmasked and true,
Face to face is where
Your light finally breaks
through.

Each glance a treasure,
a glimpse divine,
Now only infinite colors
on Your canvas shine.

Your galaxy flows
like rivers unchained,
A never-ending stream
where Your love is sustained.

Each current whispers,
each starry tide,
"I am with you, always.
Just look inside."

Deeper I wander,
yet never apart,
Forever consumed
by the depths
of Your heart.

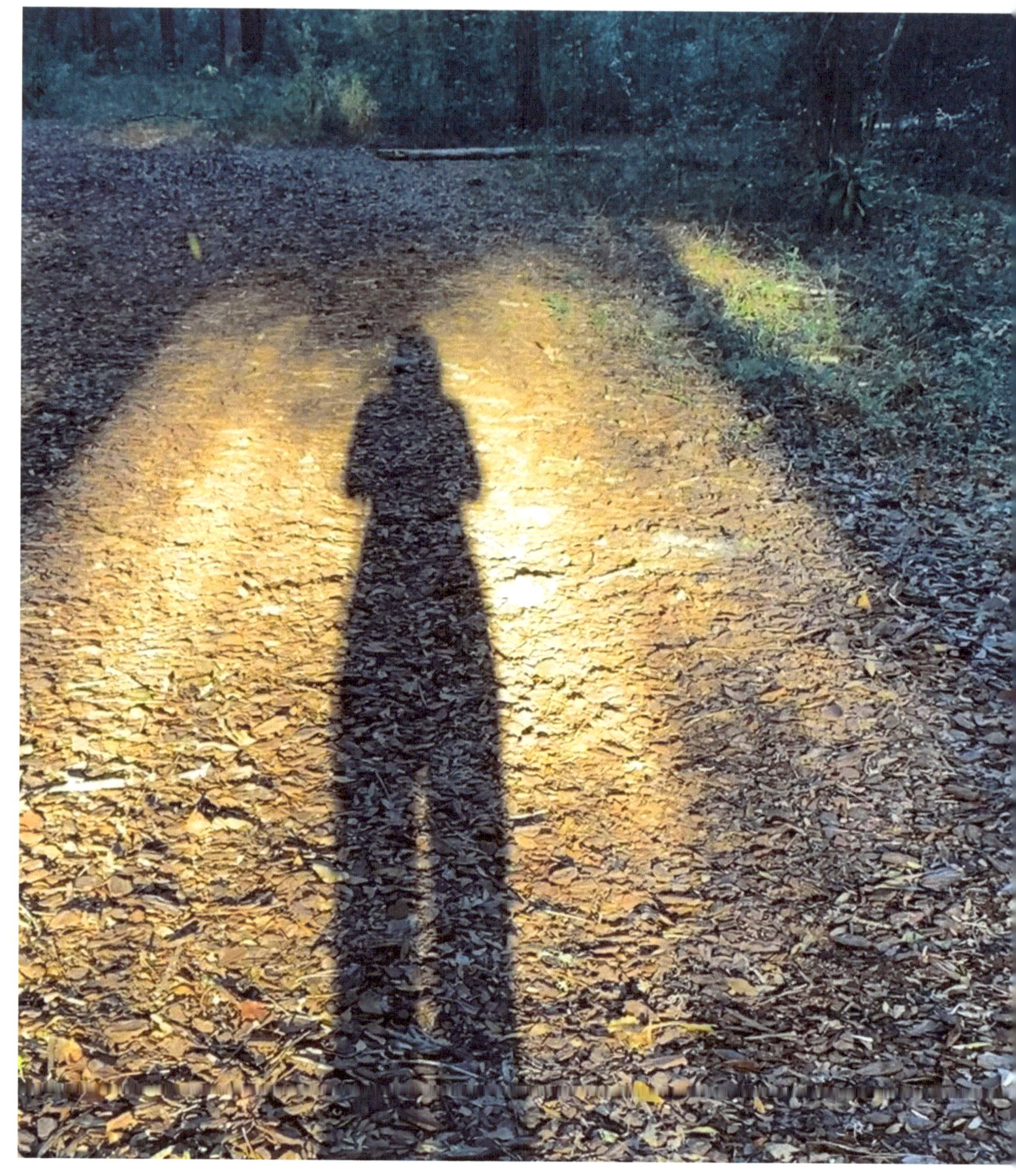

"Unseen Angels" *photography, Gainesville, FL, 2022*

angels unseen

There you were,
within my view—
What did you wonder
As I looked at you?

I was awestruck
That morning light,
Standing there stunned,
Held fast by sight.

You burned like fire
Against the ground,
Waiting patient
To be found.

A holy moment,
Laced with shock—
I stumbled onto
Sacred stock.

I didn't speak,
Just softly stood.
I need a photo—
Here, in the woods.

Your presence pierced,
A sword of flame—
It cracked me open,
It called my name.

I stood there trembling,
Split in two—
The self I was,
The self you knew.

You showed me things
I'd left unseen—
The thread of light
Behind the screen.

You never spoke,
But I was told—
In silence louder
Than the bold.

You bore the weight
I could not hold—
Standing with me
Since days of old.

You've walked beside me
From the start,
Whispering truths
Into my heart—
Clearing the way
For His great plan.

Now I see you.
Now I understand.

"For He will command His angels in regard to you, To protect and defend and guard you in all your ways [of obedience and service]. They will lift you up in their hands, So that you do not [even] strike your foot against a stone. [Luke 4:10, 11; Heb 1:14] You will tread upon the lion and cobra; The young lion and the serpent you will trample underfoot. [Luke 10:19]"Psalms 91:11-13

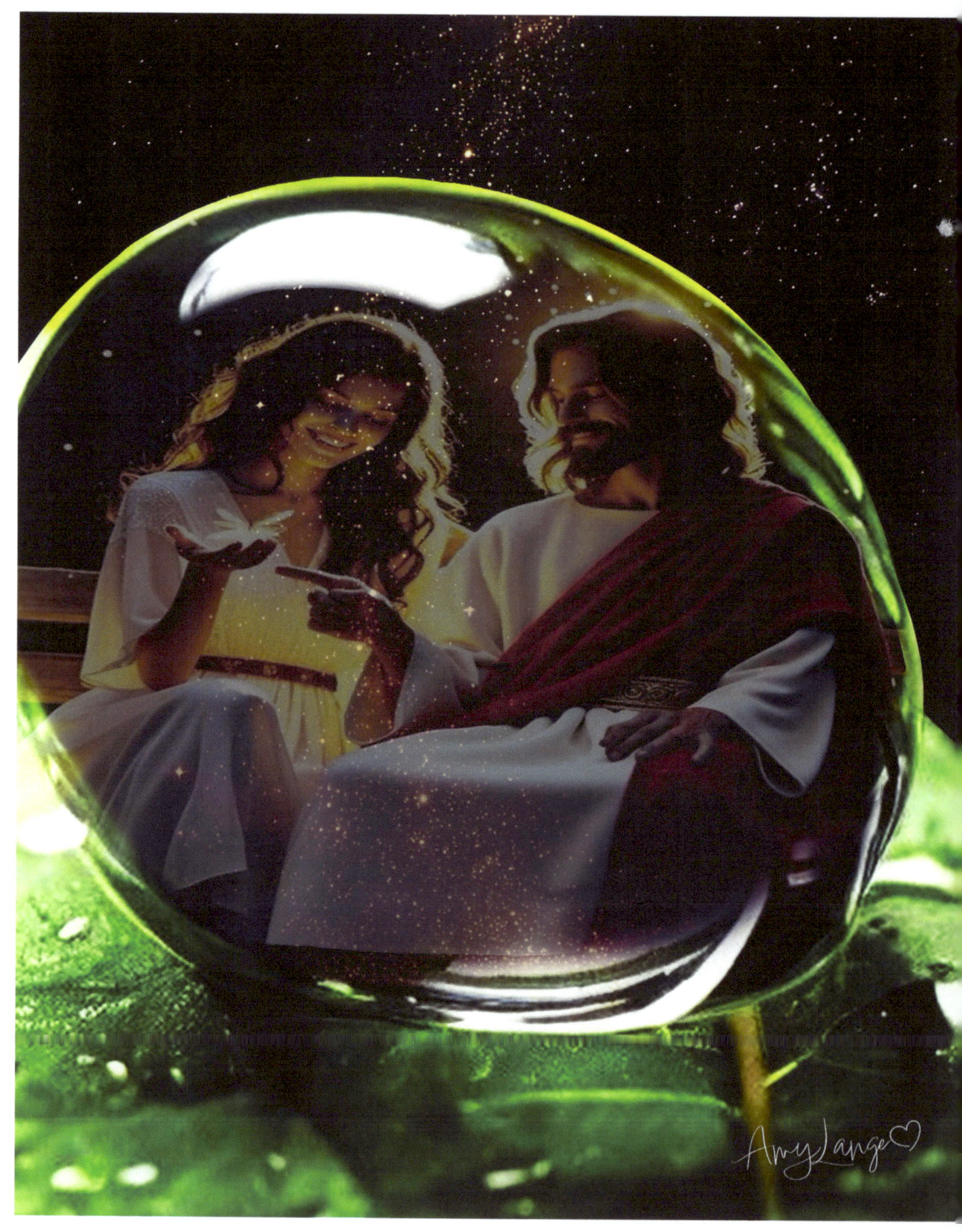

"Tiny Mysteries" *digital media*

Abba

Artist eternal,
unmatched
and supreme,
I live
in the
beauty of
Your endless
dream.

But greater
than
wonders,
both vast
and small,

You are
my Abba,
my Father,
my all.

"And so that we would know that we are His true children, God released the Spirit of Sonship into our hearts—moving us to cry out intimately, "My Father! My true Father!" Now we're no longer living like slaves under the law, but we enjoy being God's very own sons and daughters! And because we're His, we can access everything our Father has—for we are heirs because of what God has done!"
Galatians 4:6-7

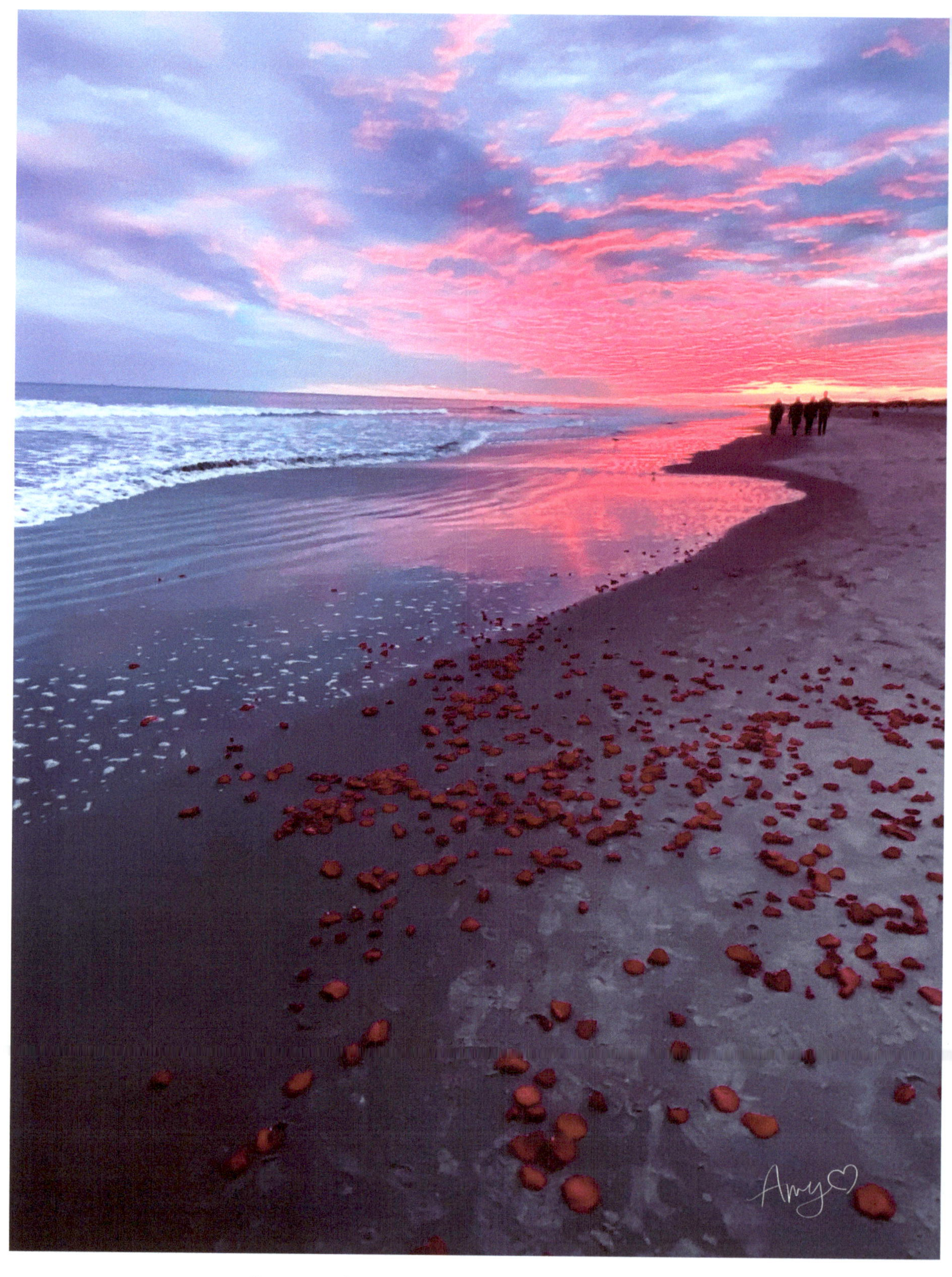

"A Kiss from Heaven" *photography, Sunset Beach, NC 2023*

a kiss from heaven

"God conceals the revelation of His word in the hiding place of His glory. But the honor of kings is revealed by how they thoroughly search out the deeper meaning of all that God says."
Proverbs 25:2

A quiet stroll
along the shore,
Where whispers hum,
and waves adore.

He paints His song
on endless skies,
A masterpiece of love
where beauty lies.

The ocean breathes
a soft embrace,
Each ripple holds
a gentle grace.

A kiss from heaven,
tender, sweet,
Where heaven and earth
in silence meet.

The flowers lay
with ocean's song,
Their petals rest
on shore as they long.

Yet time dissolves,
its pace unseen,
In moments pure
and so serene.

So here I walk,
with heart unbound,
In heaven's gift,
where peace is found.

A sacred calm,
this fleeting stay,
A kiss from heaven—
a perfect day.

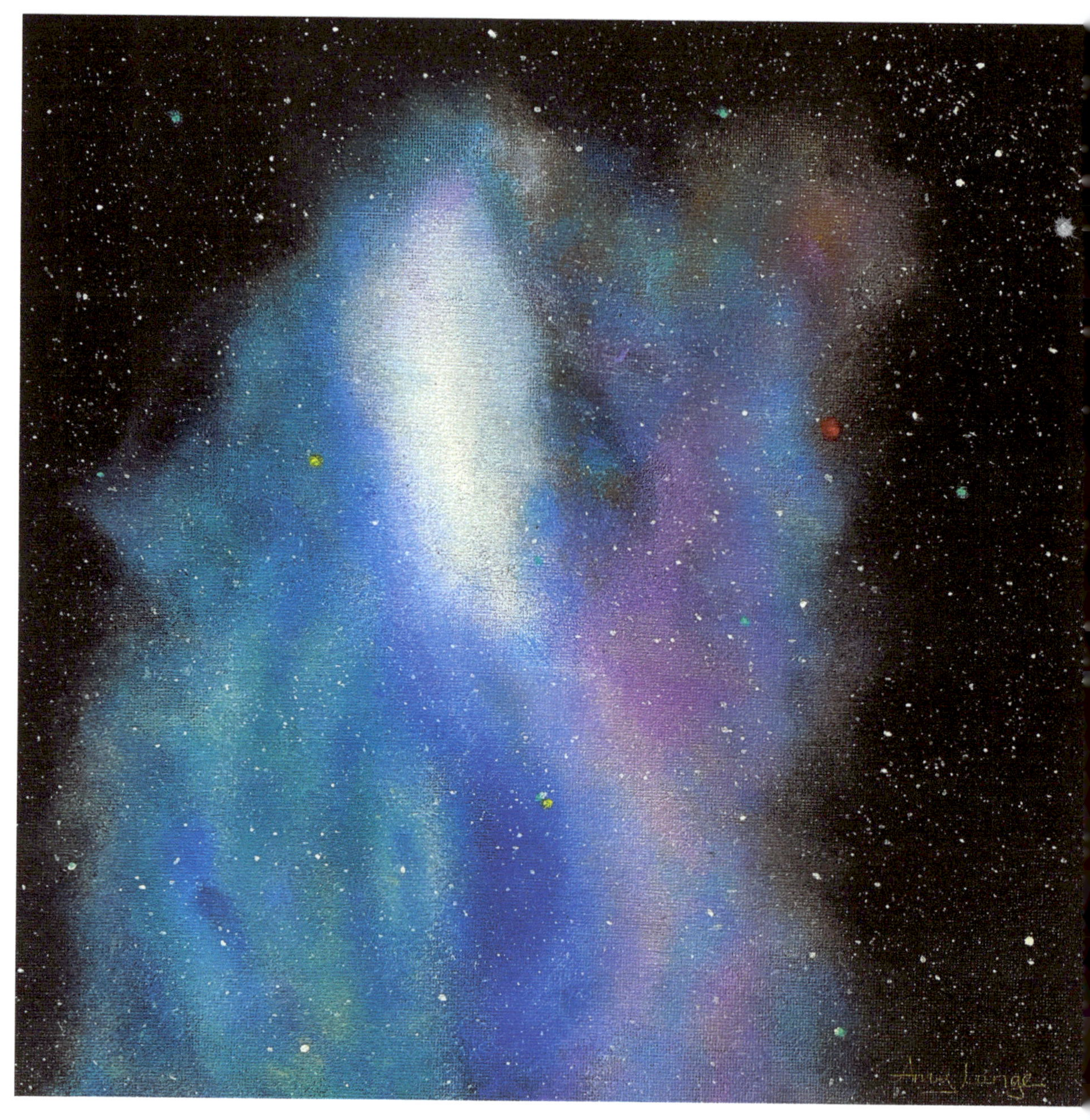

"Who Am I" *acrylic on canvas*

who am I?

All this realm
has to offer
are mere
“positions”
of power to
reflect upon ...

They are just
a window to view
distorted and
twisted fractals...
that have no matter
and no weight of gain.

Only chatter.

I am so much more
than a seat or
position of power.

So much more than
a crown of authority–
so much more than
a gavel in hand.

I have created realms
and kingdoms in Yahweh...

I stand and sit
next to the very One
Who created breath
and formed seas
without a blink.

I dance in Oneness
with the One
Who danced
with me before
the sun and moon
came to be.

I AM a king and priest
unto Yahweh
I have created worlds,
stars, cosmos and more
with my Beloved...

Together
we have governed
planets, kingdoms,
stars, orders, and more....

...all in the before.

Who Am I?
I Am as He Is...
We are
One.

"Does not wisdom call, And understanding lift up her voice? On the top of the heights beside the way, Where the paths meet, wisdom takes her stand; Beside the gates, at the entrance to the city, At the entrance of the doors, she cries out: "To you, O men, I call, And my voice is directed to the sons of men. "O you naive or inexperienced [who are easily misled], understand prudence and seek astute common sense; And, O you [closed-minded, self-confident] fools, understand wisdom [seek the insight and self-discipline that leads to godly living]. [Is 32:6] "Listen, for I will speak excellent and noble things; And the opening of my lips will reveal right things." Proverbs 8:1-6

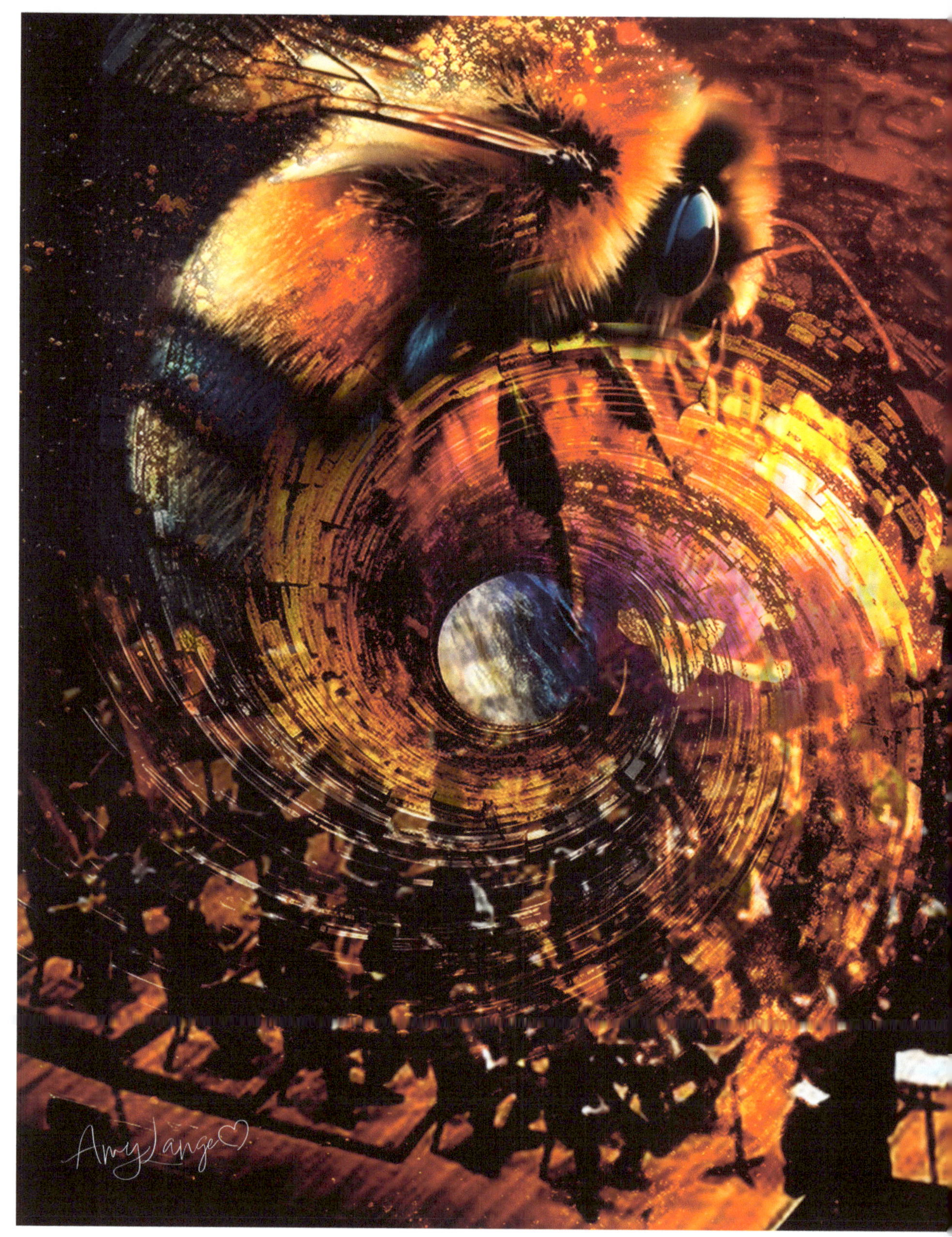

"Unseen Symphony" *digital media*

unseen symphony

"Now, this is the goal: to live in harmony with one another and demonstrate affectionate love, sympathy, and kindness toward other believers. Let humility describe who you are as you dearly love one another. Never retaliate when someone treats you wrongly, nor insult those who insult you, but instead, respond by speaking a blessing over them—because a blessing is what God promised to give you." 1 Peter 3:8-9

Oh, my sweet bee—
small to the eye,
but not to me.
I see you shimmer,
with wing-beat gleam,
a golden flicker
within the dream.

I watch you move,
I hear your song—
a hum so deep,
so wide, so strong.
You stir the soil,
you wake the air,
you spin the light
with tender care.

Tiny thing,
but mighty soul—
in you, the smallest parts
are whole.
You shift the shape
of everything,
with every beat
of fragile wing.

Never doubt
how power hides—
in quiet paths,
in gentle tides.
He lifts the world
in whispered ways,
not always loud,
but always ablaze.

It's not the mighty,
bold and tall—
but in the tiny
He moves it all.

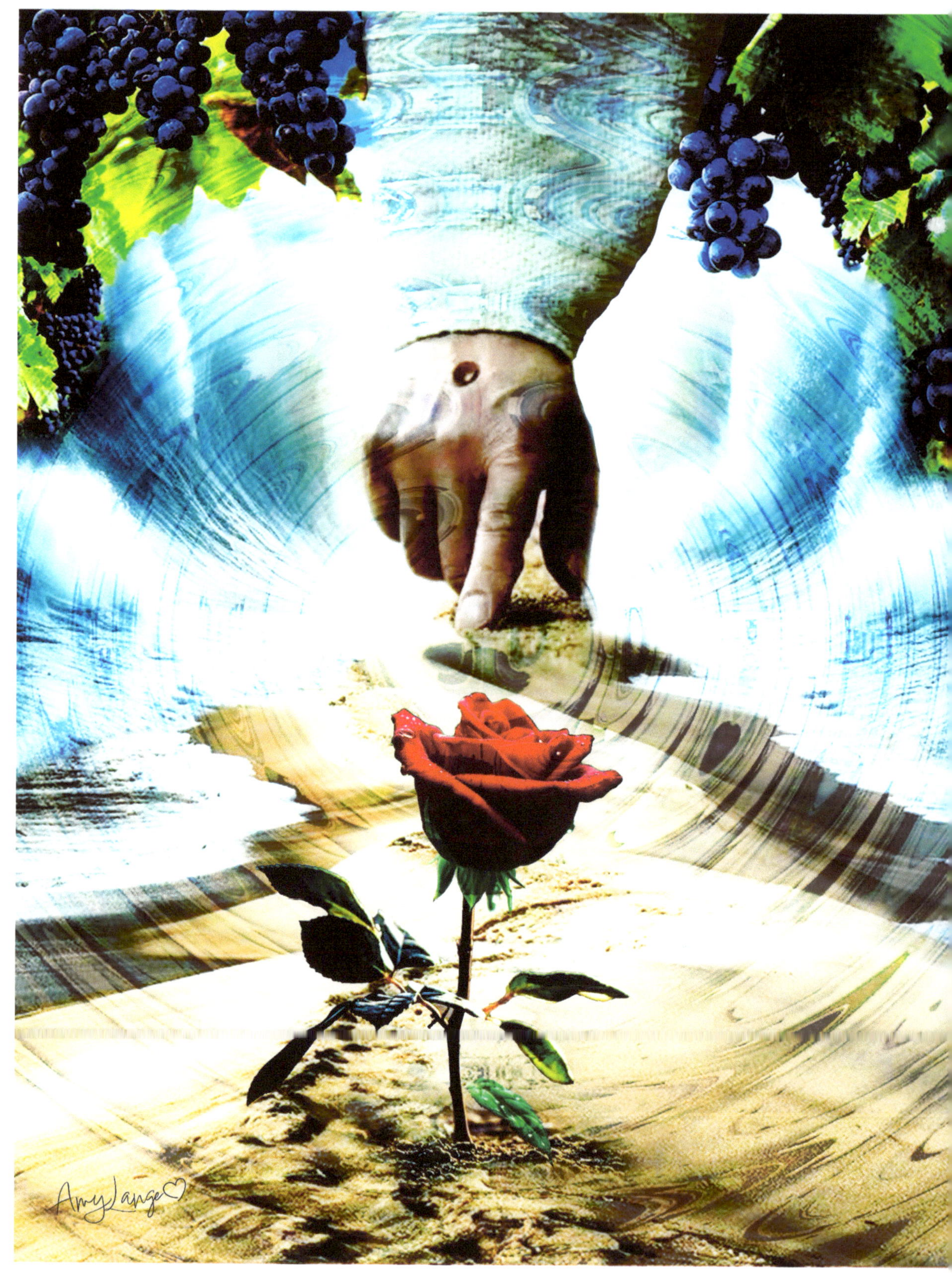

"Eternal Song" *digital media*

cross my heart

"Listen, My radiant one— if you ever lose sight of Me, just follow in My footsteps where I lead my lovers. Come with your burdens and cares. Come to the place near the sanctuary of My shepherds. My dearest one, let Me tell you how I see you— you are so thrilling to Me. To gaze upon you is like looking at one of Pharaoh's finest horses — a strong, regal steed pulling his royal chariot." Song of Songs 1:8-9

Beauty dances
in Your light,
whispers glisten,
pure and bright.

I wade into
Your living stream,
inside Your heart—
no in-between.

You take me from
the exile's clay,
through ancient years—
You are The Way.

In You alone
I'm here to stay,
Wrapped in Your love,
we dance in sway.

You are the Lamb,
who bled for me.
Now entwined,
soul at peace.

I rest beneath
Your outstretched wing—
You've crossed my heart
now I am free.

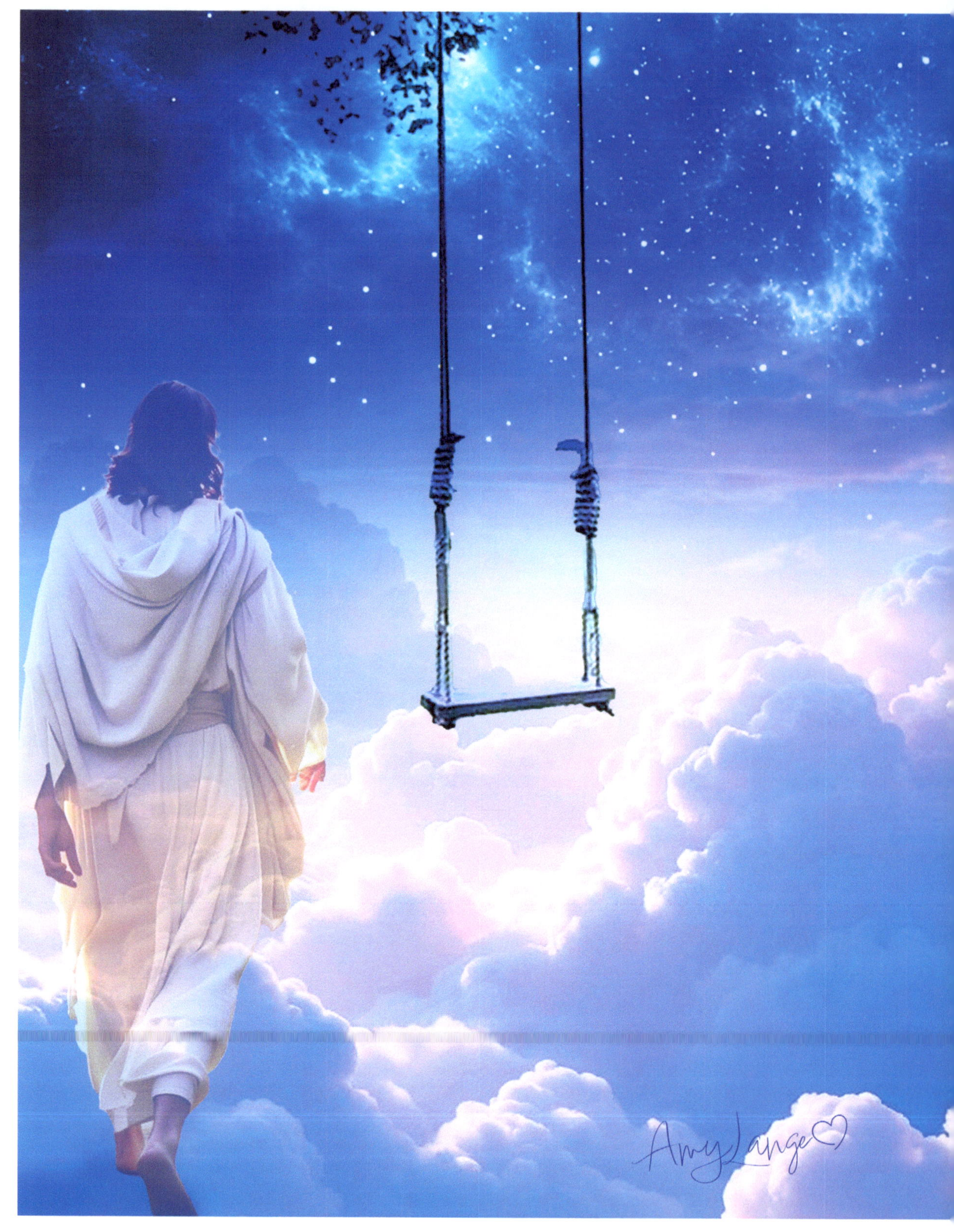

"He Woos Me" *digital media*

He woos me

Your love
calls me
into a space
Where the air
is clear,
Where the winds
embrace.

I will not waver,
my steps are set,
Hand in Yours,
No fear, nor regret.

One Way,
One sound,
One cry–
Your Crown.

"Let Him smother me with kisses—His Spirit-kiss divine. So kind are Your caresses, I drink them in like the sweetest wine! Your presence releases a fragrance so pleasing— over and over poured out. For Your lovely Name is "Flowing Oil." No wonder the brides-to-be adore You. Draw me into Your heart. We will run away together into the King's cloud-filled chamber."
Song of Songs 1:2-4

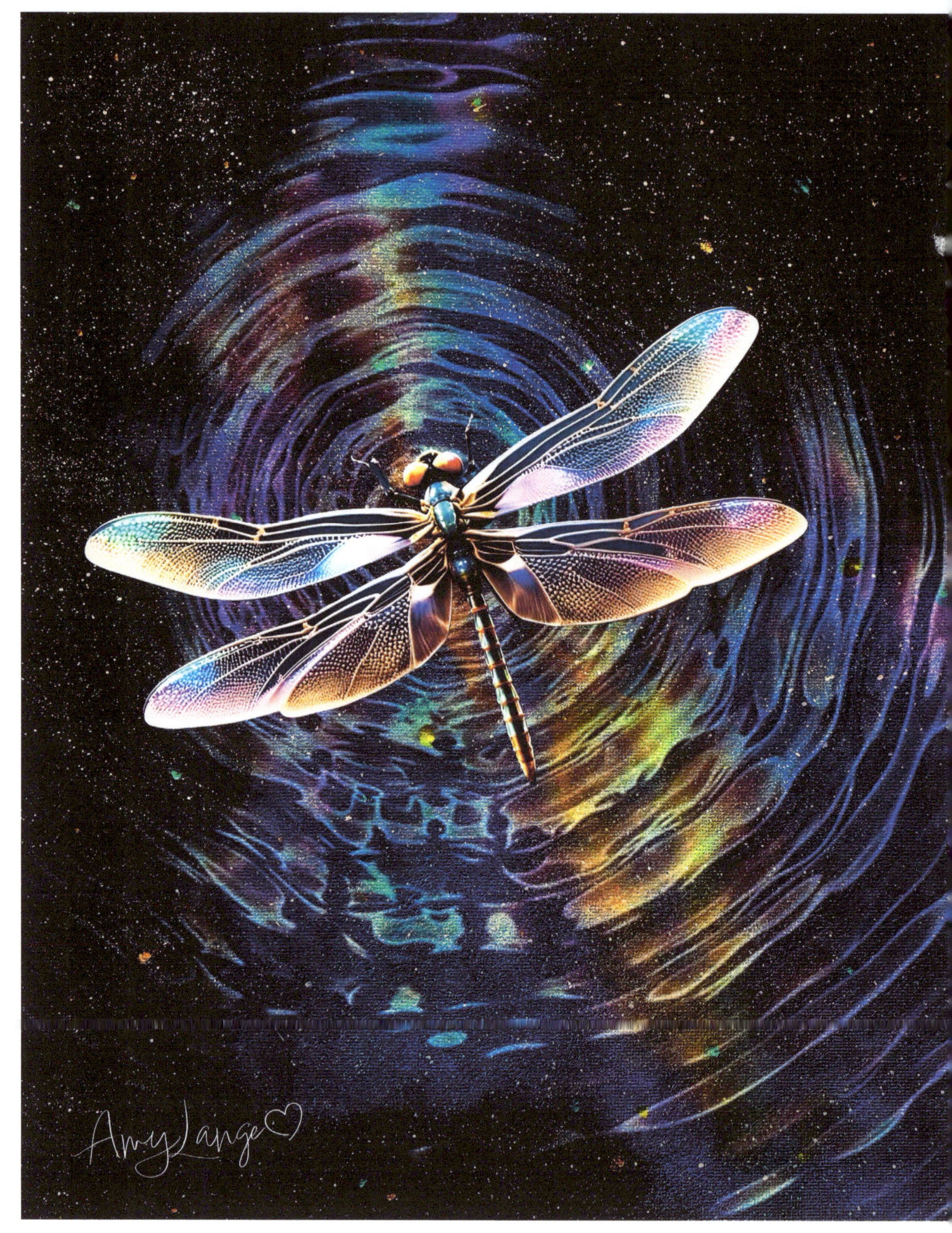

"Infinite Wonders" *mixed media*

hedged in

Fragmented thoughts
swirl and spin,
I sit here weighted,
Aching within.

Jealous fusions,
lightning strikes,
sword in hand,
words ignite.

Loveless answers,
swaying hearts,
pointing fingers,
sees in part.

Then—clear
as dawn
cutting through
the haze,
His voice
breaks in,
full of grace.

"Come away,
My darling,
come into
My deep.

Leave the clamor
and chaos,
and all things cheap.

Come where
My waters
are quiet and wide,
Come where
your questions
no longer divide.

I will show you
My face,
unhidden, unblurred—
Not in the noise,
but in every Word.

We will run
through valleys,
race over the hills,
And I will teach you
the quiet—
teach you
My still."

His kindness
wrecked me—
no turning back.
I'm diving deeply,
My soul intact.

He's my Hope,
my Anchor, my Song.
Here He sings,
here I belong.

I take His hand,
I kiss His heart.
I won't escape—
He is my part.

"Listen! I hear my Lover's voice. I know it's Him coming to me—leaping with joy over mountains, skipping in love over the hills that separate us, to come to me.

Let me describe Him: He is graceful as a gazelle, swift as a wild stag. Now He comes closer, even to the places where I hide. He gazes into my soul, peering through the portal as He blossoms within my heart."
Song of Songs 2:8-9

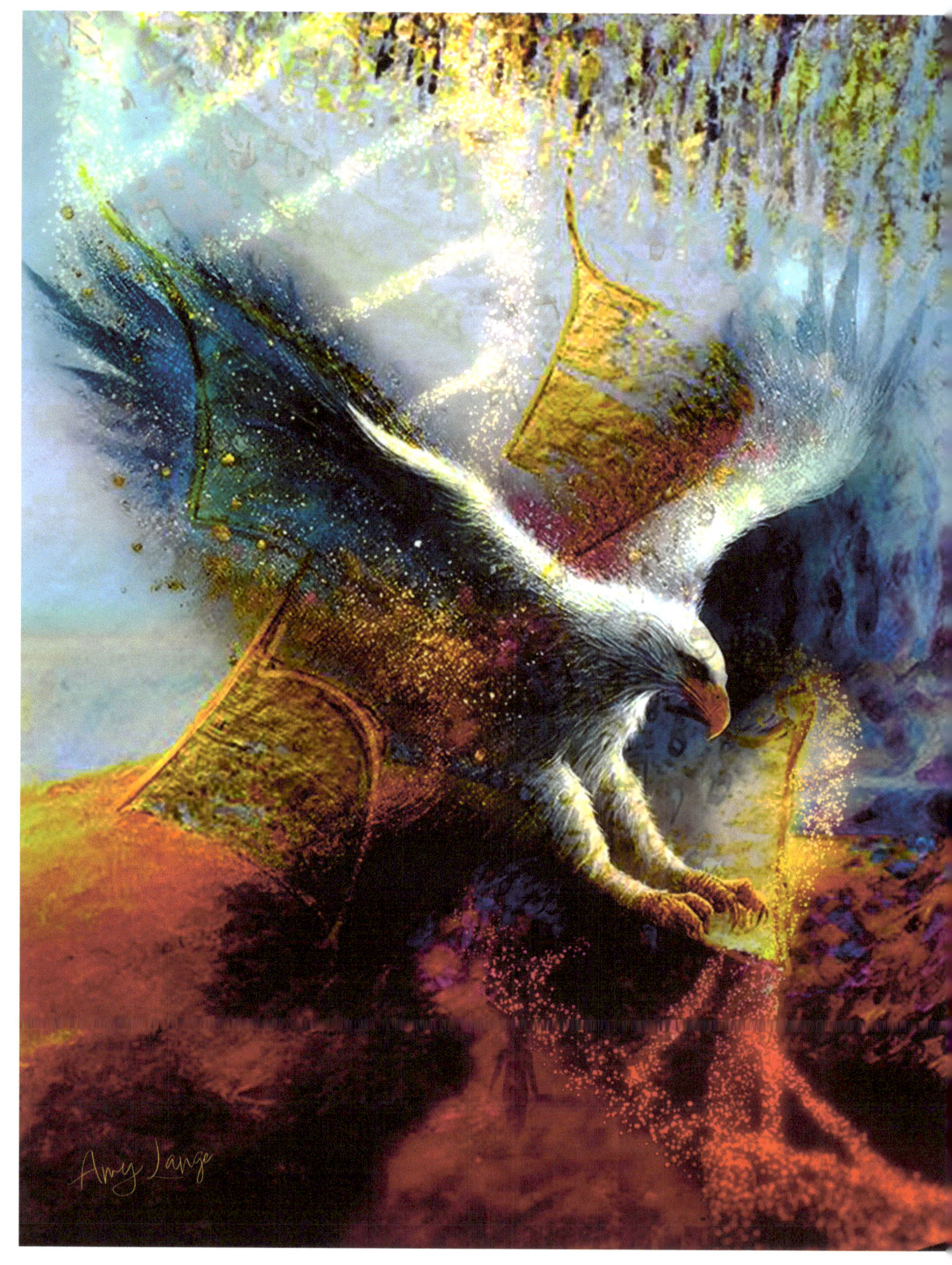

"The Wings of Aleph" *digital media*

remembering

Streaming down
from above
I sense Your grace
And Your love
In order to remember.

I walk between
The circle of time
And dance with You
In sweet sublime
And then I remember...

"My old identity has been co-crucified with Christ and no longer lives. And now the essence of this new life is no longer mine, for the Anointed One lives His life through me—We live in union as One! My new life is empowered by the faith of the Son of God who loves me so much that He gave himself for me, dispensing His life into mine!" Galatians 2:20

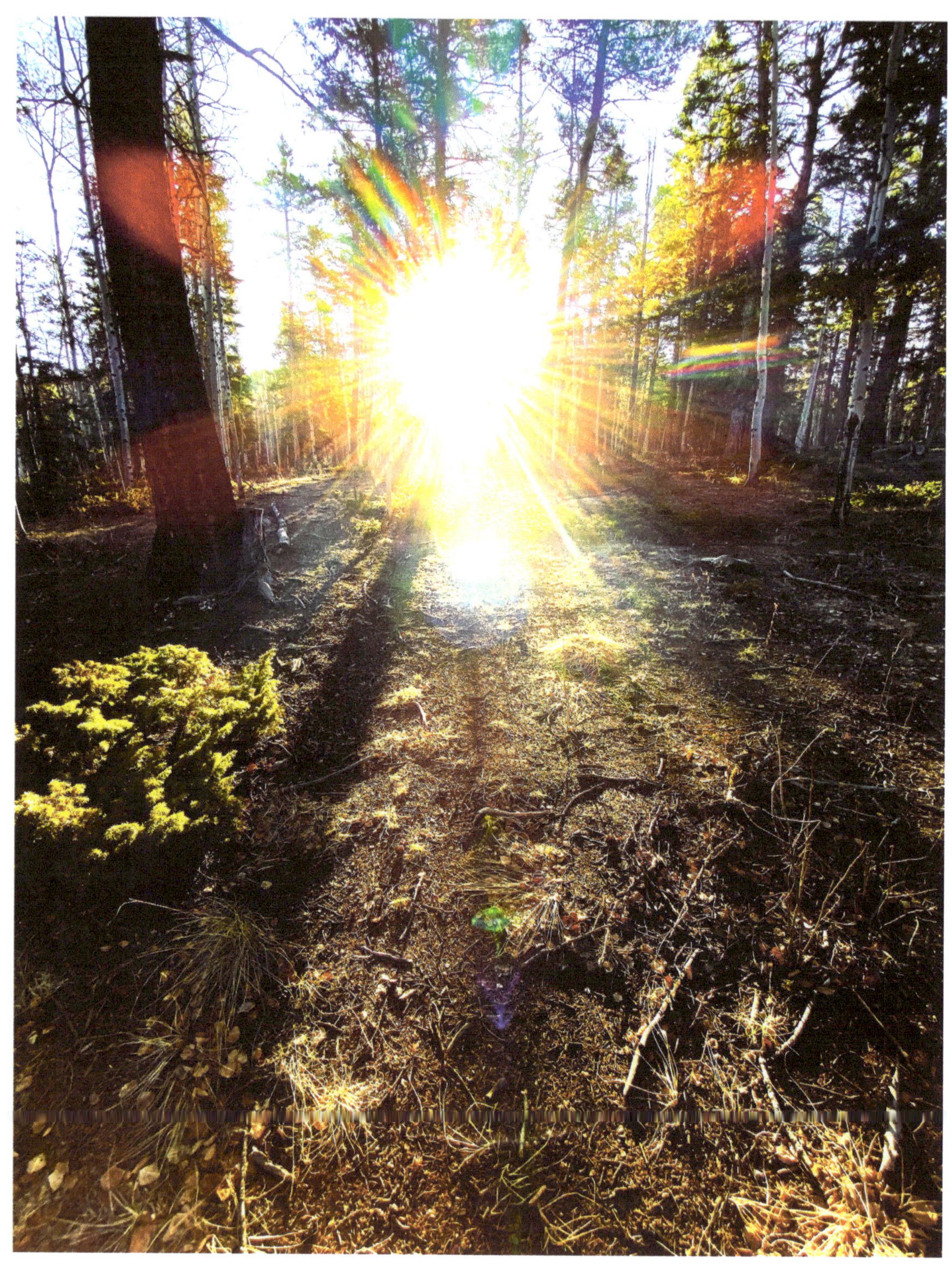

"Sacred Conversations" *photography, Pikes Peak, CO 2025*

sacred conversations

I stroll with You
Along the path
Hand in hand
In light I bask.

Amid the buzz
Of cars surround
I quiet my soul
To hear Your sound.

Your whispers take me
To a place
Where creation stirs
And nature awakes.

Closer I lean
Into Your heart,
Time stands still,
No end, no start.

Your presence enfolds
Like light unseen,
A whisper felt,
Both strong and serene.

No need for words,
No need for sound,
Lost in Your love
"I Am" I'm found

*"Awake, O north wind!
Awake, O south wind!*

Breathe on my garden with Your Spirit-Wind. Stir up the sweet spice of Your life within me. Spare nothing as You make me Your fruitful garden. Hold nothing back until I release Your fragrance.

Come walk with me as You walked with Adam in your paradise garden. Come taste the fruits of Your life in me."
Song of Songs 4:16

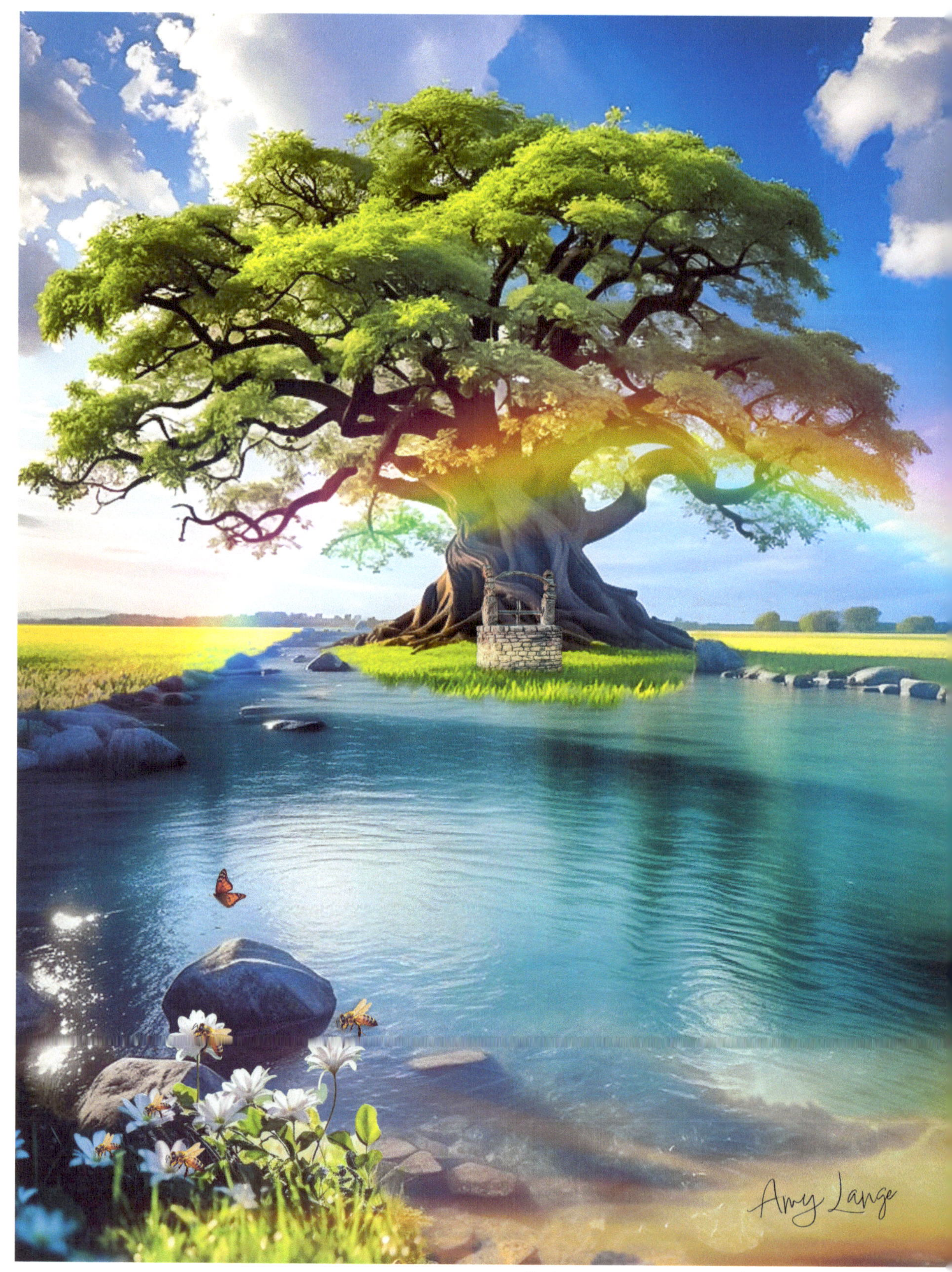

"Shevat HaChaim" *digital media*

pause. breathe. be.

Press pause,
don't hit play.
Press pause,
begin your day.

Press pause,
sit and breathe.
Press pause,
simply be.

Time keeps moving,
rushing past,
but stillness waits
beyond the fast.

Press pause,
the NOW is vast.

"He offers a resting place for me in His luxurious love. His tracks take me to an oasis of peace near the quiet brook of bliss. That's where He restores and revives my life. He opens before me the right path and leads me along in His footsteps of righteousness so that I can bring honor to His name. Even when Your path takes me through the valley of deepest darkness, fear will never conquer me, for You already have! Your authority is my strength and my peace. The comfort of Your love takes away my fear. I'll never be lonely, for You are near. You become my delicious feast even when my enemies dare to fight. You anoint me with the fragrance of your Holy Spirit; You give me all I can drink of You until my cup overflows!
Psalms 23:2-5

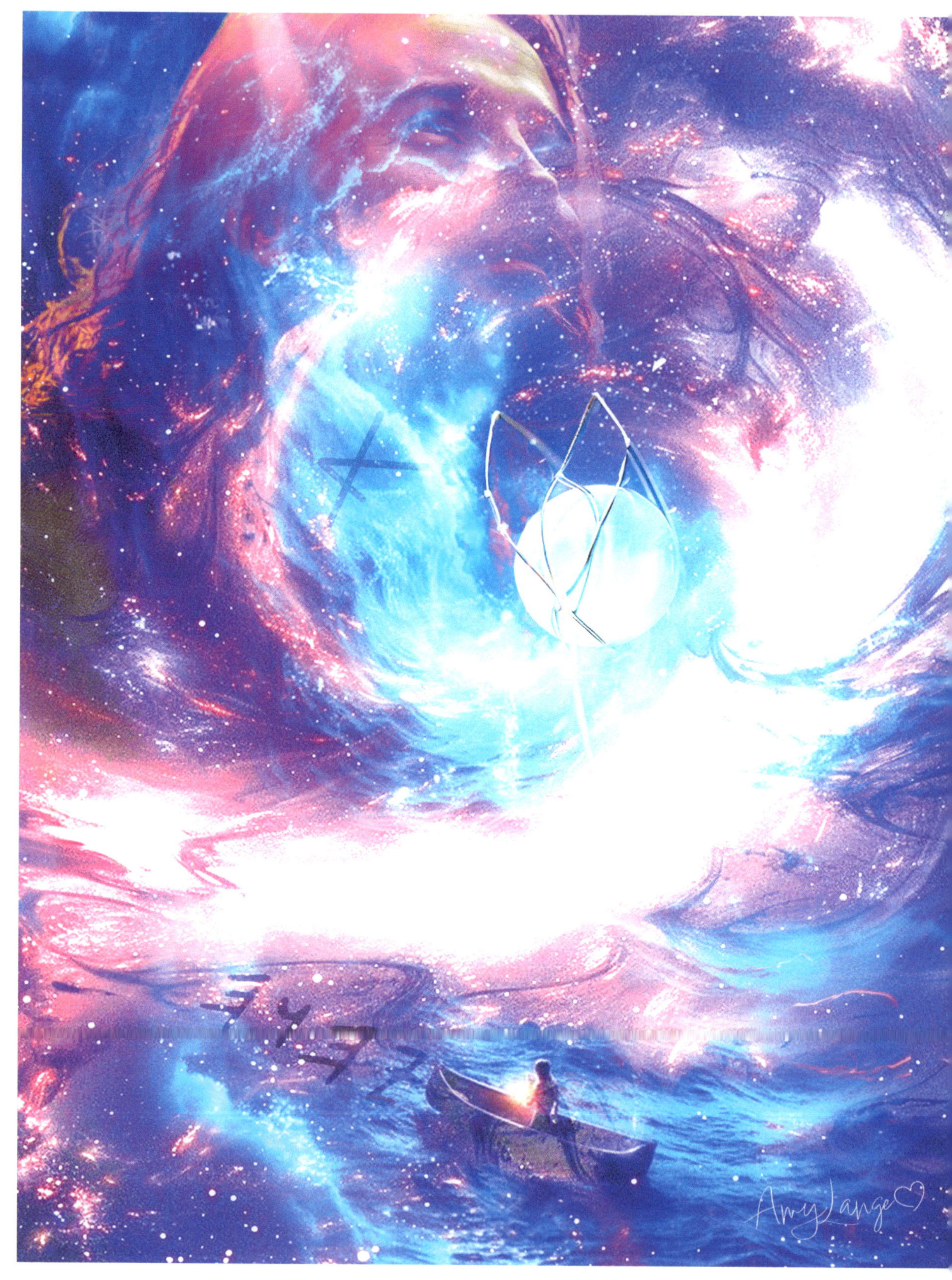

"I Am Enough" *digital media*

I Am enough

Restless soul,
aching, worn—
chasing dreams
lost in storm.

I hear a voice,
so still, so small,
calling faintly
through the fog:
"I Am Enough."

His door is low,
yet oh, so divine,
love overflowing,
endlessly mine.

I bury my face,
shedding my tears,
pouring my heart out—
I know He hears.

Through the night,
through rising fear,
a whisper breaks:
"I'm always near.
I Am Enough."

My heart is broken,
yet never lost.
Now it is His,
no matter the cost.

I will follow Your heart
into the deep,
You've captured my gaze
and step of my feet.

The tides of Your love
have swept me away,
turning my heart
day after day.

Above the waves,
above the din,
a voice calls out,
again, again:
"I Am Enough."

And like the shore
to the endless sea,
You are now mine—
woven into me.

You are enough.

"God, You're such a safe and powerful place to find refuge! You're a proven help in time of trouble—more than enough and always available whenever I need You.

So we will never fear even if every structure of support were to crumble away. We will not fear even when the earth quakes and shakes, moving mountains and casting them into the sea. For the raging roar of stormy winds and crashing waves cannot erode our faith in You.

Pause in His presence" Psalms 46:1-3

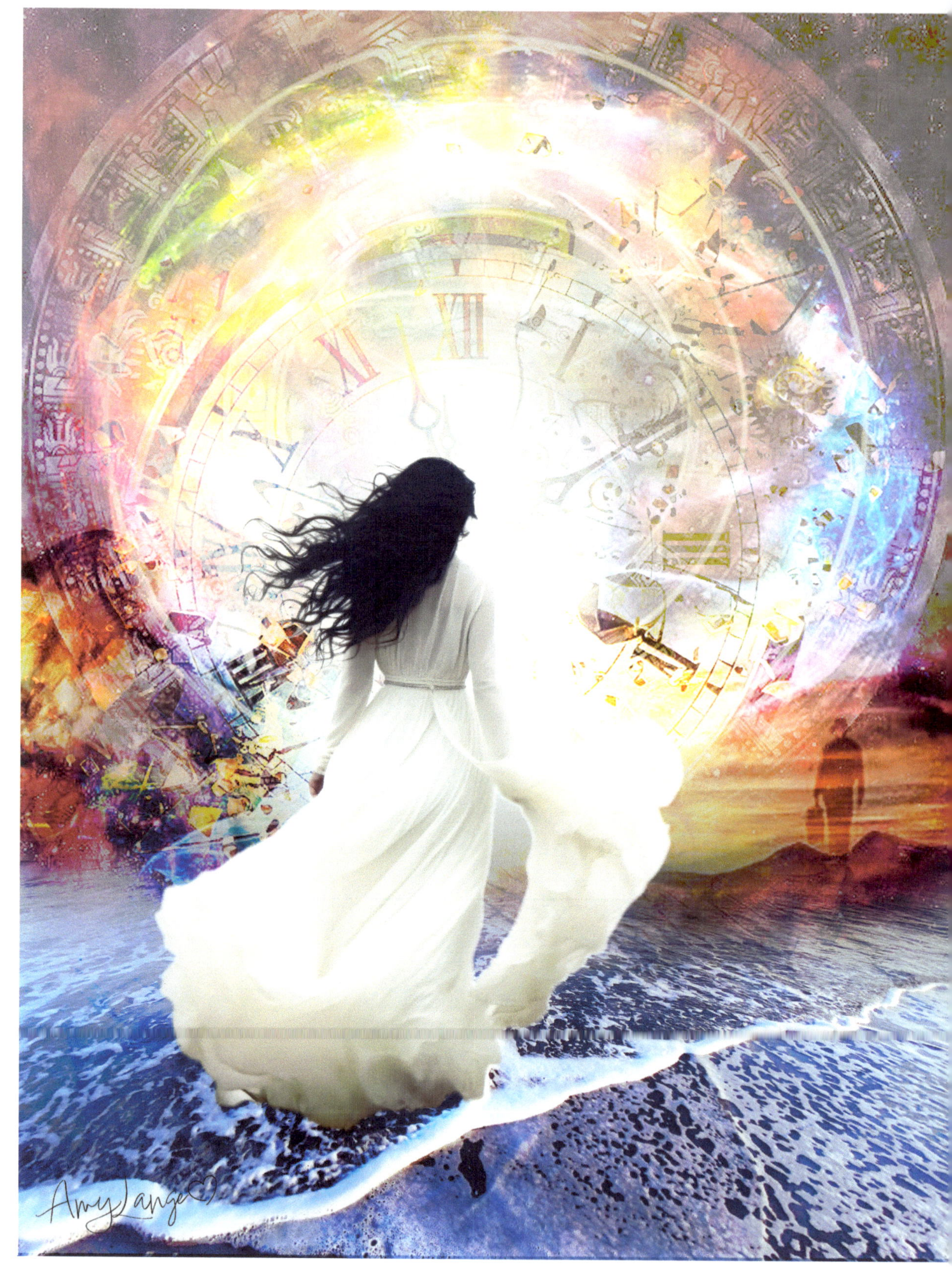

"The Collide of Time" *digital media*

the fog

I'm confined
by fleeting boundaries,
shadows pressing near.
I see with measured vision,
but never what is clear.

My heart and mind are swirling–
where do I turn my clock?
To the left lies only anguish,
hidden in the dock.

To the right, a golden sunrise–
a promise soft yet thin.
Is it guiding me to glory,
or luring me again?

Oh, fog, why do you linger?
My heart resists your stay.
If only you could measure
the faith that lights my way.

"...Overwhelmed with bliss are all who will entwine their hearts in Him, waiting for Him to help them. Yes, the people of Zion who live in Jerusalem will weep no more. How compassionate He will be when He hears your cries for help! He will answer you when He hears your voice! Even though the Lord may allow you to go through a season of hardship and difficulty, He himself will be there with you. He will not hide Himself from you, for your eyes will constantly see Him as your Teacher. When you turn to the right or turn to the left, you will hear His voice behind you to guide you, saying, "This is the right path; follow it."" Isaiah 30:18-21

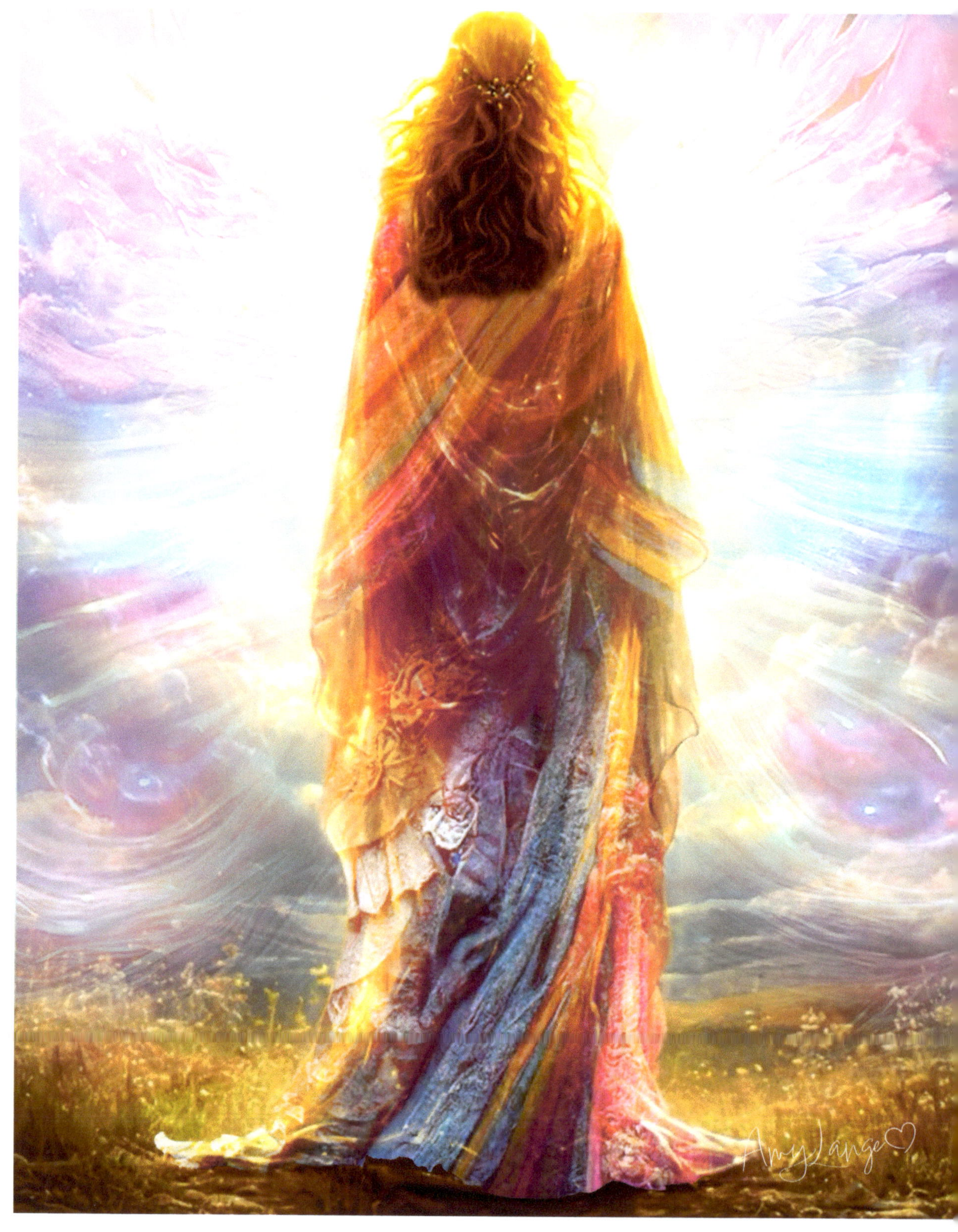

"Threaded By Heaven" *digital media*

threaded by heaven

Behold!
I wear a coat.
Ancient.
Sacred.
Specific–
Made for me.

Threaded with
mystery,
so intricate,
so exquisitely
designed by divinity.

Its size is
unlike any other–
tailor-made
by God Himself.

Inlaid
with diamonds,
shimmering
with light,
a rainbow
of heaven–
I am my
Father's delight.

Woven
with destiny,
hidden from
the eyes of man.
Only the humble
catch a glimpse
of what
He has planned.

The colors
declare me.
They blaze
without shame–
not for show,
not for pride.
For His glory,
I was placed
in time.

I am my
Father's daughter.
He has given
me this coat.
I wear it.
I walk in it.
I live in it–fully.

I am chosen.
I am loved.
I am seen.
He is mine.

Wear your coat.

"O my beloved, you are lovely. When I see you in your beauty, I see a radiant city where We will dwell as One. More pleasing than any pleasure, more delightful than any delight, you have ravished My heart, stealing away My strength to resist you. Even hosts of angels stand in awe of you. The shining of your spirit shows how you have taken My truth to become balanced and complete. Your beautiful blushing cheeks reveal how real your passion is for Me, even hidden behind your veil of humility. I could have chosen any from among the vast multitude of royal ones who follow Me. But unique is My beloved dove–unrivaled in beauty, without equal, beyond compare, the perfect one, the favorite one. Others see your beauty and sing of your joy. Brides and queens chant your praise: "How blessed is she!" Look at you now– arising as the dayspring of the dawn, fair as the shining moon, bright and brilliant as the sun in all its strength–astonishing to behold as a majestic army waving banners of victory." Song of Songs 6:4, 6-10

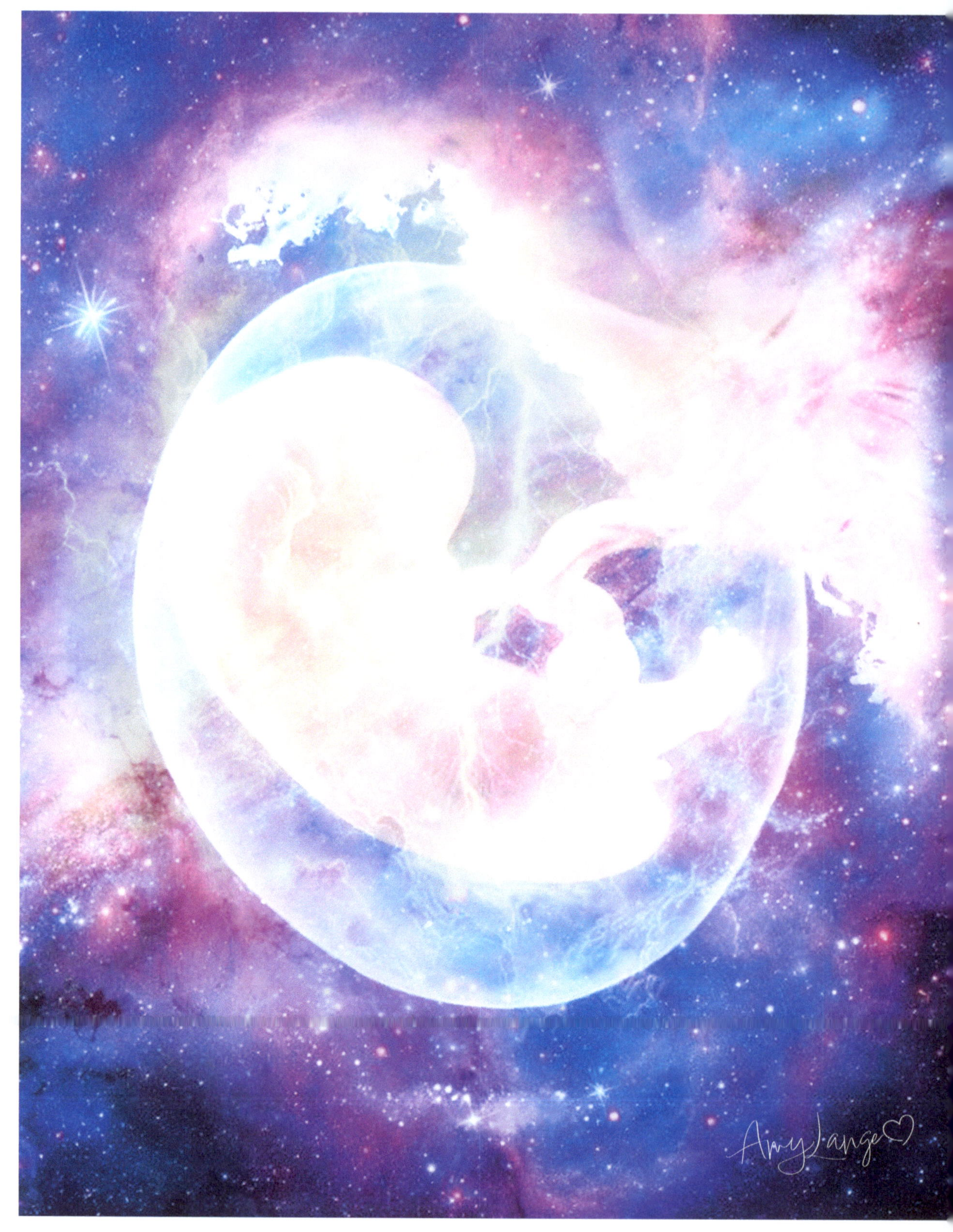

"Unbridled Love" *digital media*

unbridled love

Who can understand
the thunder of
Your power?

Your voice
transcends
all boundaries—
my existence
is confined
to Your breath—
my air.

In compassion,
You hold me.
My frame You keep
from tearing apart,
fragile as I am.

You whisper
with the hush
of stars,
delighting over me
like One who
sees treasure
in broken things.

Gently You lead me—
Drawing me close,
Never by force
Hiding me beneath
the shadow
of Your wings,
You woo me
to Your beat
The sweetest sound—
Your eternal heart.

Your ways—
untraceable.
Your power—
capable of ruin.
And yet You choose
to preserve me.
To guide me
with a hand
that could
shatter stone
but instead
writes mercy.

Your force—
unmatched.
Your glory—
a weight no soul
can bear,
a sound collapsing
all creation.

Still, You stoop
to catch the faintest cry
of a child
lost in the dark.

Who can know
Your depths?
Who can understand?

My breath
rests in You,
in the shelter
of Your name—

Yah-weh.

"You are so intimately aware of me, Lord. You read my heart like an open book and You know all the words I'm about to speak before I even start a sentence! You know every step I will take before my journey even begins. You've gone into my future to prepare the way, and in kindness You follow behind me to spare me from the harm of my past. You have laid your hand on me! This is just too wonderful, deep, and incomprehensible! Your understanding of me brings me wonder and strength. Where could I go from Your Spirit? Where could I run and hide from Your face?" Psalms 139:3-7

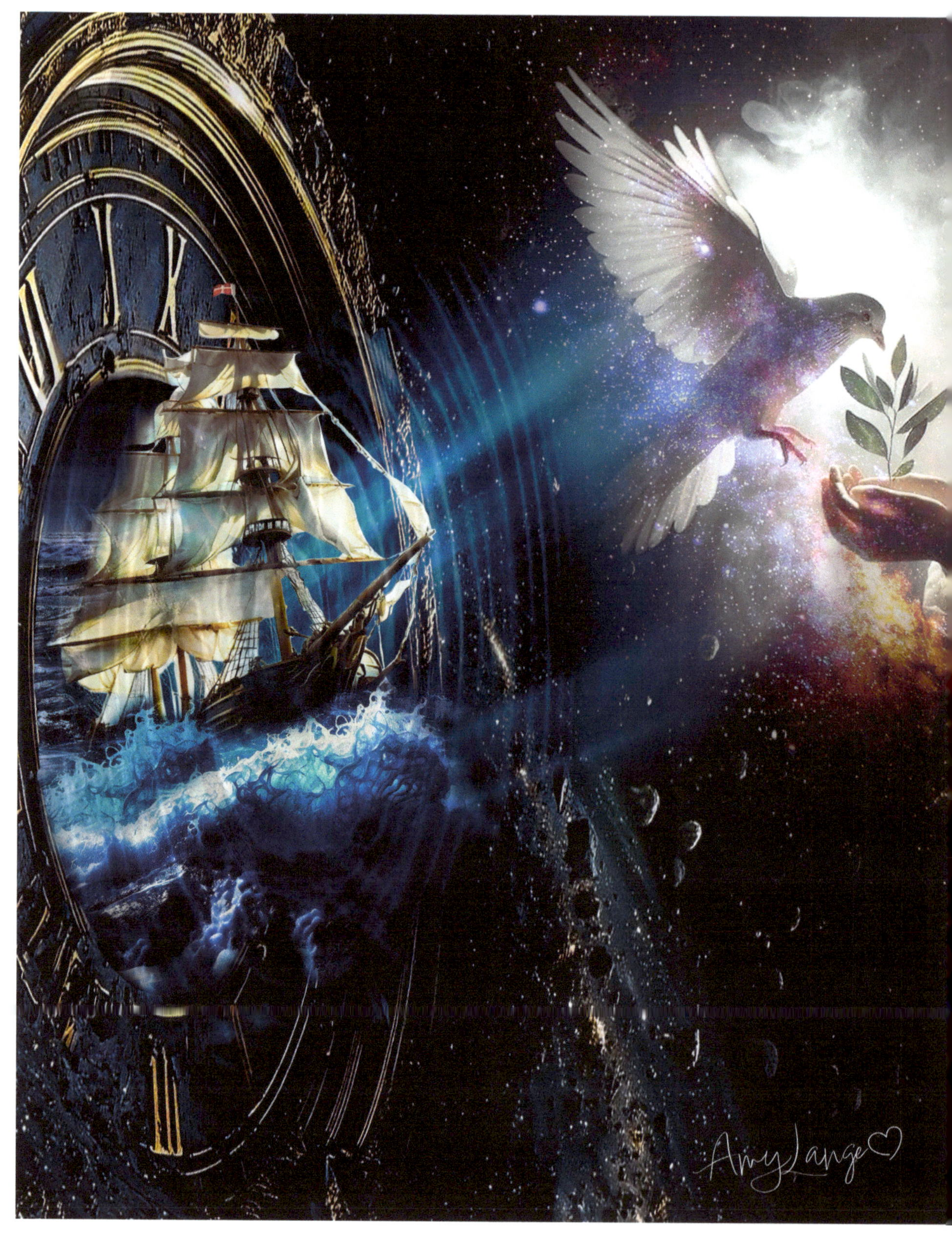

"CHRONOS in the Crosswind" *digital media*

First Love

"The words I have spoken over you have already cleansed you. So you must remain in life-union with Me, for I remain in life-union with you. For as a branch severed from the vine will not bear fruit, so your life will be fruitless unless you live your life intimately joined to Mine."
John 15:3-4

While the ages are colliding,
an unseen force
moves through the air,
to change her course.

It lures the Bride to drink
its wine—
Whispering "take a sip,
You'll be just fine."

Gears are turning,
Alarms go off.
The end draws near—
and scoffers scoff.
But in the lull,
the Bride's asleep—
tottering to each side—
she's in too deep.

What is she drunk with,
you may ask?
She's poured the world
into her flask.

She eats, she drinks,
she buys and sells,
Consumed by earth's
whistles and bells.
Drunk with pleasures,
drunk with wine,
Drunk in the swirls
of the times.

Within the Bride,
both great and small,
Few see the ruin
beneath it all.
They laugh and squander,
yet do not see
Jesus bleeding on a tree.

They've left His heart,
and now comes strife—
division cuts
through every life.
A house divided
will not stand—
its fall is written
by its own hand.

Still He stands
and cries once more:
"Will My Bride
remember
I'm knocking
at her door?"

Woe to you, merchants—
your hour is done.
In one swift turn,
your time has come.

All earthen treasures
will never compare
to His beauty, His dance—
so rich, so rare.

In one swift move,
You claim Your Bride.
The earth is shaken
as You kiss Your wife.

I'm undone
and awakened by
Your joy and life—
Your breath is a river,
restoring inside.

You bubble up within,
we move beyond time.

I drink deeply of Your love—
so much richer than wine.
Oh, how I love You
my Beloved, mine.

arcing with eternity

When Jesus becomes your Savior—
He also becomes your Healer.
Your Redeemer.
Your Wonderful Counselor.
Your Mighty God.
Your Prince of Peace.
The Everlasting.
Your Great Shepherd.
Husband. Brother. Bridegroom.
The Way. The Truth. The Life.
The Word. The Breath.
Faith. Hope. Love...
and infinitely more.

When He steps inside of you,
Its more than acknowledgement—
you suddenly carry Him.
The infinite Healer.
The faithful Counselor.
The power of Heaven itself
living inside
your mortal body.
You are
immortal.

In a moment—
you shift realms.
From darkness... to Light.

What once held you
is driven out.
Darkness flees.
Chains explode.
Sickness collapses.
Death is devoured.

Why?
Because all of Heaven
now burns within you.

"In the beginning was the Word, and the Word was with God, and the Word was God. He was in the beginning with God. All things were made through Him, and without Him nothing was made that was made. In Him was life, and the life was the light of men." John 1:1-4

"And the light shines in the darkness, and the darkness did not comprehend it." John 1:5

The Word—
who became flesh
and walked among us—
now lives inside of you.

The Lion of Judah
roars inside your chest.
The Spirit of the Living God
fills your lungs
with holy breath.
Your heartbeat
thunders and arcs
with eternity.

You are no longer
a prisoner of shadows—
you are a carrier of His fire.
Every step you take
pushes back the night.
Every word you speak
streams with His
resurrection
power.

Darkness trembles
when the eyes
of your heart open.
The grave remembers
it has no claim on you.
You are His.

For Light shines in the darkness—
and darkness cannot remain.

Your body—now His sacred dwelling.
You thought you knew what love was...
but this Love
is fire and flood,
gentle and fierce,
utterly consuming,
beyond anything you could
ever experience in the natural.

From within, He whispers
with the voice that
shaped the stars—

"Come away with Me, My darling.
Let us run through the hills
with delight.
Delight yourself in Me."

The risen Christ has
taken hold of you.
Every shackle of darkness
has fallen away.
His Light—
He is Light.
Christ in you—
the Hope of Glory!

Scriptures

"In the beginning God created the heavens and the earth. The earth was unformed and void, darkness was on the face of the deep, and the Spirit of God hovered over the surface of the water. Then God said, "Let there be light"; and there was light. God saw that the light was good, and God divided the light from the darkness." **Genesis1:1-4**

"Rise up in splendor and be radiant, for your light has dawned, and Yahweh's glory now streams from you! Look carefully! Darkness blankets the earth, and thick clouds covers the nations, but Yahweh arises upon you and the brightness of his glory appears over you!" **Isaiah 60:1-2**

"Call to Me and I will answer you, and tell you [and even show you] great and mighty things, [things which have been confined and hidden], which you do not know and understand and cannot distinguish." **Jeremiah 33:3**

"Because of You, I know the path of life, as I taste the fullness of joy in Your presence. At Your right side I experience divine pleasures forevermore." **Psalms 16:11**

"Listen to my counsel, for my instruction will enlighten you. You'll be wise not to ignore it. If you wait at wisdom's doorway, longing to hear a word for every day, joy will break forth within you as you listen for what I'll say. For the fountain of life pours into you every time that you find me, and this is the secret of growing in the delight and the favor of the Lord." **Proverbs 8:33-35**

"Behold, I'm standing at the door, knocking. If your heart is open to hear my voice and you open the door within, I will come in to you and feast with you, and you will feast with me." **Revelation 3:20**

"Stop dwelling on the past. Don't even remember these former things. I am doing something brand new, something unheard of. Even now it sprouts and grows and matures. Don't you perceive it? I will make a way in the wilderness and open up flowing streams in the desert." **Isaiah 43:18-19**

"[You are the One] who covers Yourself with light as with a garment, Who stretches out the heavens like a tent curtain, Who lays the beams of His upper chambers in the waters [above the firmament], Who makes the clouds His chariot, Who walks on the wings of the wind, Who makes winds His messengers, Flames of fire His ministers. [Heb 1:7]" **Psalms 104:2-4**

"For He will command His angels in regard to you, To protect and defend and guard you in all your ways [of obedience and service]. They will lift you up in their hands, So that you do not [even] strike your foot against a stone. [Luke 4:10, 11; Heb 1:14] You will tread upon the lion and cobra; The young lion and the serpent you will trample underfoot. [Luke 10:19]" **Psalms 91:11-13**

"And so that we would know that we are His true children, God released the Spirit of Sonship into our hearts—moving us to cry out intimately, "My Father! My true Father!" Now we're no longer living like slaves under the law, but we enjoy being God's very own sons and daughters! And because we're His, we can access everything our Father has—for we are heirs because of what God has done!" **Galatians 4:6-7**

"God conceals the revelation of His word in the hiding place of His glory. But the honor of kings is revealed by how they thoroughly search out the deeper meaning of all that God says." **Proverbs 25:2**

"Does not wisdom call, And understanding lift up her voice? On the top of the heights beside the way, Where the paths meet, wisdom takes her stand, Beside the gates, at the entrance to the city, At the entrance of the doors, she cries out: "To you, O men, I call, And my voice is directed to the sons of men. "O you naive or inexperienced [who are easily misled], understand prudence and seek astute common sense; And, O you [closed-minded, self-confident] fools, understand wisdom [seek the insight and self-discipline that leads to godly living]. [Is 32:6] "Listen, for I will speak excellent and noble things; And the opening of my lips will reveal right things." **Proverbs 8:1-6**

"Now, this is the goal: to live in harmony with one another and demonstrate affectionate love, sympathy, and kindness toward other believers. Let humility describe who you are as you dearly love one another. Never retaliate when someone treats you wrongly, nor insult those who insult you, but instead, respond by speaking a blessing over them–because a blessing is what God promised to give you." **1 Peter 3:8-9**

"Listen, My radiant one– if you ever lose sight of Me, just follow in My footsteps where I lead my lovers. Come with your burdens and cares. Come to the place near the sanctuary of My shepherds. My dearest one, let Me tell you how I see you– you are so thrilling to Me. To gaze upon you is like looking at one of Pharaoh's finest horses – a strong, regal steed pulling his royal chariot." **Song of Songs 1:8-9**

"Let Him smother me with kisses–His Spirit-kiss divine. So kind are Your caresses, I drink them in like the sweetest wine! Your presence releases a fragrance so pleasing– over and over poured out. For Your lovely Name is "Flowing Oil." No wonder the brides-to-be adore You. Draw me into Your heart. We will run away together into the King's cloud-filled chamber." **Song of Songs 1:2-4**

"Listen! I hear my Lover's voice. I know it's Him coming to me– leaping with joy over mountains, skipping in love over the hills that separate us, to come to me.

Let me describe Him: He is graceful as a gazelle, swift as a wild stag. Now He comes closer, even to the places where I hide. He gazes into my soul, peering through the portal as He blossoms within my heart." **Song of Songs 2:8-9**

"My old identity has been co-crucified with Christ and no longer lives. And now the essence of this new life is no longer mine, for the Anointed One lives His life through me–We live in union as One! My new life is empowered by the faith of the Son of God who loves me so much that He gave himself for me, dispensing His life into mine!" **Galatians 2:20**

"Awake, O north wind! Awake, O south wind!

Breathe on my garden with Your Spirit-Wind. Stir up the sweet spice of Your life within me. Spare nothing as You make me Your fruitful garden. Hold nothing back until I release Your fragrance.

Come walk with me as You walked with Adam in your paradise garden. Come taste the fruits of Your life in me." **Song of Songs 4:16**

"He offers a resting place for me in His luxurious love. His tracks take me to an oasis of peace near the quiet brook of bliss. That's where He restores and revives my life. He opens before me the right path and leads me along in His footsteps of righteousness so that I can bring honor to His name. Even when Your path takes me through the valley of deepest darkness, fear will never conquer me, for You already have! Your authority is my strength and my peace. The comfort of Your love takes away my fear. I'll never be lonely, for You are near. You become my delicious feast even when my enemies dare to fight. You anoint me with the fragrance of your Holy Spirit; You give me all I can drink of You until my cup overflows!" **Psalms 23:2-5**

"God, You're such a safe and powerful place to find refuge! You're a proven help in time of trouble– more than enough and always available whenever I need You.

So we will never fear even if every structure of support were to crumble away. We will not fear even when the earth quakes and shakes, moving mountains and casting them into the sea. For the raging roar of stormy winds and crashing waves cannot erode our faith in You.

Pause in His presence" **Psalms 46:1-3**

"...Overwhelmed with bliss are all who will entwine their hearts in Him, waiting for Him to help them. Yes, the people of Zion who live in Jerusalem will weep no more. How compassionate He will be when He hears your cries for help! He will answer you when He hears your voice! Even though the Lord may allow you to go through a season of hardship and difficulty, He himself will be there with you. He will not hide Himself from you, for your eyes will constantly see Him as your Teacher. When you turn to the right or turn to the left, you will hear His voice behind you to guide you, saying, "This is the right path; follow it."" **Isaiah 30:18-21**

"O my beloved, you are lovely. When I see you in your beauty, I see a radiant city where We will dwell as One. More pleasing than any pleasure, more delightful than any delight, you have ravished My heart, stealing away My strength to resist you. Even hosts of angels stand in awe of you. The shining of your spirit shows how you have taken My truth to become balanced and complete. Your beautiful blushing cheeks reveal how real your passion is for Me, even hidden behind your veil of humility. I could have chosen any from among the vast multitude of royal ones who follow Me. But unique is My beloved dove–unrivaled in beauty, without equal, beyond compare, the perfect one, the favorite one. Others see your beauty and sing of your joy. Brides and queens chant your praise: "How blessed is she!" Look at you now– arising as the dayspring of the dawn, fair as the shining moon, bright and brilliant as the sun in all its strength– astonishing to behold as a majestic army waving banners of victory." **Song of Songs 6:4, 6-10**

"You are so intimately aware of me, Lord. You read my heart like an open book and You know all the words I'm about to speak before I even start a sentence! You know every step I will take before my journey even begins. You've gone into my future to prepare the way, and in kindness You follow behind me to spare me from the harm of my past. You have laid your hand on me! This is just too wonderful, deep, and incomprehensible! Your understanding of me brings me wonder and strength. Where could I go from Your Spirit? Where could I run and hide from Your face?" **Psalms 139:3-7**

"The words I have spoken over you have already cleansed you. So you must remain in life-union with Me, for I remain in life-union with you. For as a branch severed from the vine will not bear fruit, so your life will be fruitless unless you live your life intimately joined to Mine." **John 15:3-4**

"In the beginning was the Word, and the Word was with God, and the Word was God. He was in the beginning with God. All things were made through Him, and without Him nothing was made that was made. In Him was life, and the life was the light of men." **John 1:1-4**

"And the light shines in the darkness, and the darkness did not comprehend it." **John 1:5**

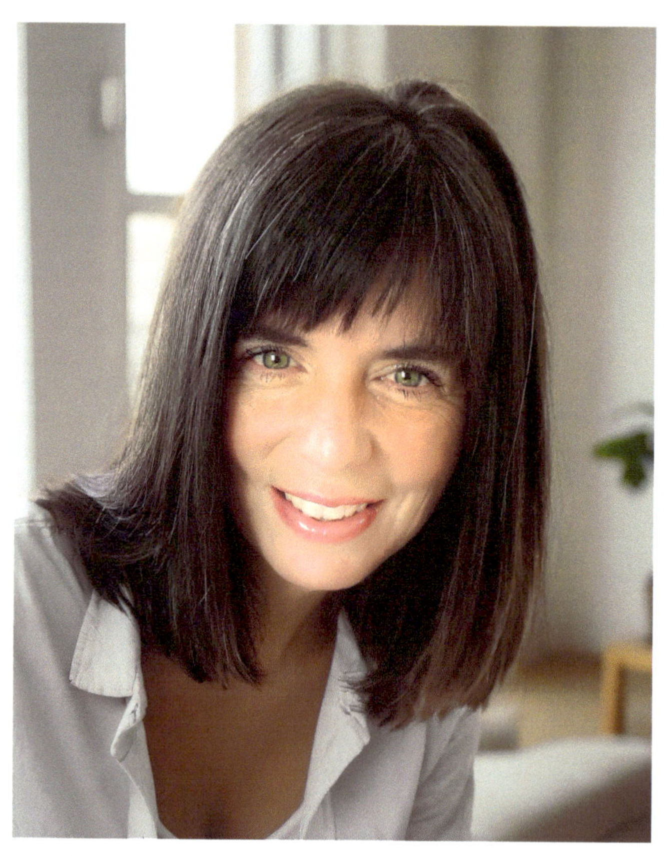

ABOUT THE AUTHOR

Amy Lange is a revivalist through and through. While many church-age terms have grown familiar, Amy carries a heart to see them rewritten—with fresh vision and meaning for what Yahweh is releasing in the earth today. Because revive means "to restore to life or consciousness, to resuscitate," her desire is for the Bride to awaken—to receive His breath and arise in identity and authority, in alignment with Isaiah 60.

In 2022, Holy Spirit commissioned Amy and her two children on a cross-country journey to pray over cities and regions across America. For three years, they lived on the road, following His lead and praying wherever He sent them—preparing the ground and hearts for what He is doing.

Amy's favorite thing is finding tiny kisses from heaven each day. She loves spending time in nature, watching sunrises and sunsets, adventuring on bike trails, taking long walks on the beach, or simply sitting by a cozy fire with her favorite tea. Most of all, she loves being a mom to her two incredible children.

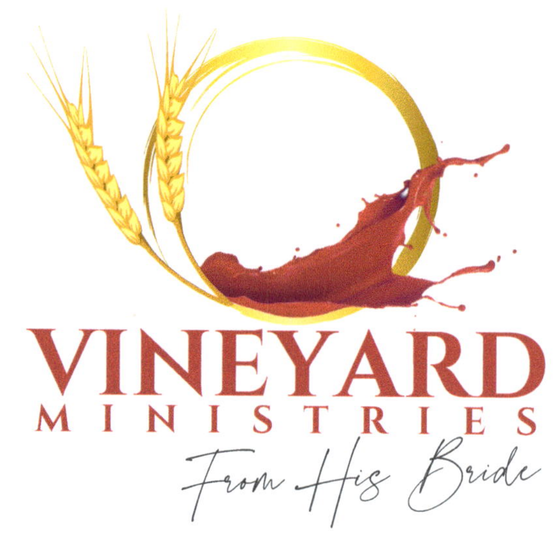
VINEYARD
MINISTRIES
From His Bride

VINEYARD MINISTRIES FROM HIS BRIDE

Amy recently launched *Vineyard Ministries From His Bride* (www.vineyardministries.one) under the direction of Holy Spirit, creating space for others who carry the same longing to gather together and respond. Her heart is to move with Holy Spirit and release His new wine for the harvest, as He sends her into cities and regions to individuals, leaders, groups, and ministries. Her desire is not for a fresh "outpour" as in the days of old, but for the deep wells within the Bride to break open and gush forth—igniting intimacy and longing for her Bridegroom once again.

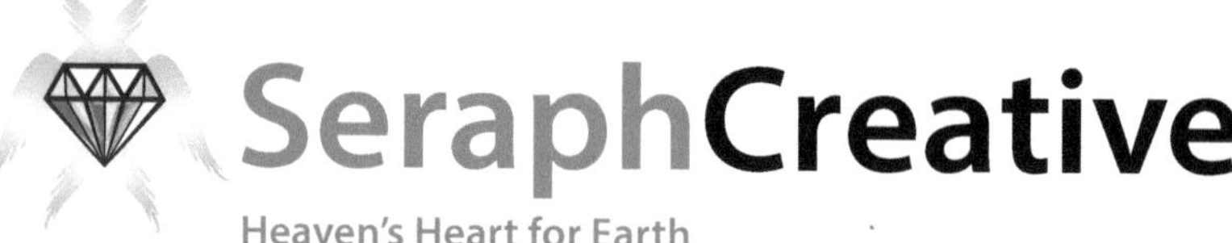

Seraph Creative is a collective of artists, writers, theologians & illustrators who desire to see the body of Christ grow into full maturity, walking in their inheritance as Sons of God on the Earth.

Sign up to our newsletter to know about future exciting releases.

Visit our website: www.seraphcreative.org

www.ingramcontent.com/pod-product-compliance
Ingram Content Group UK Ltd.
Pitfield, Milton Keynes, MK11 3LW, UK
UKHW060116300726
14090UKWH00002B/224

* 9 7 8 1 9 6 4 9 5 9 7 0 2 *